Profess

Teaching and Assessing Skills in
Accounting

Catherine Coucom

Learning Resource Centre
Georgian College
One Georgian Drive
Barrie, ON
L4M 3X9

CAMBRIDGE UNIVERSITY PRESS

CAMBRIDGE UNIVERSITY PRESS
Cambridge, New York, Melbourne, Madrid, Cape Town, Singapore, São Paulo

Cambridge University Press
The Edinburgh Building, Cambridge CB2 2RU, UK

www.cambridge.org
Information on this title: www.cambridge.org/9780521543675

© University of Cambridge International Examinations 2005

This book is in copyright. Subject to statutory exception
and to the provisions of relevant collective licensing agreements,
no reproduction of any part may take place without
the written permission of Cambridge University Press.

First published 2005

Printed in the United Kingdom at the University Press, Cambridge

A catalogue record for this publication is available from the British Library

ISBN-13 978-0-521-54367-5 paperback
ISBN-10 0-521-54367-3 paperback

ACKNOWLEDGEMENTS
All sample IGCSE questions are reproduced from University of Cambridge
International Examinations past examination papers.

Cambridge University Press has no responsibility for the persistence or
accuracy of URLs for external or third-party Internet websites referred to in
this book, and does not guarantee that any content on such websites is, or
will remain, accurate or appropriate.

Contents

Foreword		iv
1	Introduction	1
2	Practical considerations	3
3	The role of skills in Accounting	21
4	Teaching skills in Accounting	31
5	Assessing skills in Accounting	51
6	Preparing students for Accounting examinations	61
7	Conclusion	68
Appendix A:	Useful textbooks	69
Appendix B:	Useful addresses	71
Appendix C:	Examples of assessments	73
Appendix D:	Key (command) words in Accounting examinations	83
Appendix E:	Answers to teacher activities	85
Index		89

Foreword

Teaching is a complex and demanding profession. All over the world societies change in response to new knowledge gained, technological developments, globalisation and a requirement for an ever more sophisticated and educated population. Teachers are in the forefront of such social change, responding with speed and confidence to the new demands made of them, both in terms of their knowledge and of the way in which they teach. This series is intended to help them in adapting to these changes and in their professional development as teachers.

Curriculum changes worldwide are putting increased emphasis on the acquisition of skills as well as subject knowledge, so that students will be able to respond flexibly to the swiftly changing modern environment. As a result, teachers must be able to teach and assess skills and to adjust their own teaching methods to embrace a wider range of techniques for both teaching and assessing in the classroom. The books in this series are practical handbooks which explore these techniques and offer advice on how to use them to enhance the teacher's own practice.

The handbooks are written by teachers with direct experience of teaching and assessing skills at this level. We have asked them to write for their readers in such a way that the readers feel directly supported in their professional development. Thus, as well as tasks for students, there are tasks for teachers, pauses for reflection and questions to be answered. We hope that readers will find that this mixture of the practical and the professional helps them, both in their practice and in their own sense of what it means to be an effective teacher in this modern, changing world of international education.

Dr Kate Pretty
Series Editor

1 Introduction

'Who was Luca Pacioli?' asked one of the speakers at a recent accountants' seminar.

Surprisingly, none of the delegates had heard of the man regarded by many as the father of double entry book-keeping.

Luca Pacioli, a Franciscan friar, who lived in Venice in the fifteenth century, was a professor of mathematics. His book on the principles of mathematics – *Summa de arithmetica, geometria, proportioni et proportionalita* – also included a section in which the general principles of double entry were formulated. It is believed that double entry book-keeping existed long before the fifteenth century, but that Luca Pacioli was the first person to actually explain the system in a published work. In the *Summa* he wrote:

> It is necessary that all a businessman's affairs be arranged in a systematic way so that he may get their particulars at a glance ... without systematic recording, their minds would always be so tired and troubled that it would be impossible for them to conduct business.

This is still relevant in the world of business today. The information provided by accounting records is invaluable for the operating of any business, irrespective of whether that business consists of a sole trader or a multinational concern.

The accounting profession has a very long and proud history and has played a vital part in the world of business for centuries. There is no doubt that young people entering the profession today find it much more interesting than did their predecessors of even 20 years ago. Technology has transformed the basic manual, repetitive functions of accounting into a computer-led process. It is still important, however, for those studying accounting to understand the entries being made by these computer programs and the purpose of such entries.

The skills our students acquire during their course of study provide the foundation on which they can build a very rewarding career in the world of business. We, as teachers of Accounting, are privileged to be able to help our students develop a unique set of skills. Studying Accounting aids the development of such skills as orderliness and logical thought processes. These disciplines will remain with the students long after they leave school or college and will be of benefit in every walk of life.

I am sure that we all take great pleasure in following the careers of our past students. It is immensely satisfying to learn of their success at university or in accountancy examinations. Simply comparing the knowledge of Accounting students at the end of the course with their complete lack of subject knowledge at the start of the course is rewarding for the teacher. The information and instruction provided by the teacher during the course is evidenced by the students' ability to use technical accounting terms correctly, prepare ledger accounts, cash books, final accounts, and so on.

This book is primarily aimed at teachers who are preparing students for introductory examinations in Accounting such as IGCSE or O level. Whether you are new to teaching, or are an experienced teacher, I hope this book will stimulate you to think about your teaching methods and offer ideas which you can develop for use with your classes.

In Chapter 2 I have tried to address practical issues such as the learning environment and resources for both students and teachers. The aims and objectives of syllabuses are discussed, together with how they can be converted into schemes of work. Chapter 3 concentrates on the skills which students of Accounting need to acquire, and how those skills can be integrated. Different ways in which accounting skills can be taught are covered in Chapter 4. This chapter also contains lesson plans and learning activities. Chapter 5 is concerned with the different ways in which students' progress can be assessed. The practical aspects of preparing students for Accounting examinations are discussed in Chapter 6.

Every classroom situation is different, and the experience of every teacher is different, so there are, necessarily, many different ways of teaching Accounting. This book is based on my own experiences over many years as a teacher and examiner. The activities suggested in this book have worked well with my own students, but may need to be adapted for use with your students. They are offered as illustrations of different approaches to teaching the same topics, based on student participation in the lessons, and encouraging understanding of the various topics within the syllabus.

2 Practical considerations

The learning environment
When the timetable has been drawn up, teachers can begin to plan for the forthcoming school year. Before you consider schemes of work and lesson plans, it is worth giving some thought to the practical issues such as the classroom and the resources available.

The classroom
Will you be based in your own classroom, with the students coming to you, or will you move to different classrooms for each lesson? If you have your own room, it is possible to arrange the layout to suit your own requirements. You will probably have the opportunity to use display boards for any posters you are able to produce or obtain. It may also be possible to store equipment such as overhead projectors and board rulers in the room rather than having to transport them each time they are required.

This may not be possible if you are holding your classes in different classrooms. You may find that rooms are not ideally suited to your requirements, but, unfortunately, sometimes this has to be accepted. Many schools are short of classrooms and conditions are not always ideal for the learning environment.

One thing which is essential is plenty of board space – a traditional chalk board, or a whiteboard. Consider working an exercise on the board which involves a cash book, ledger (divided into general, purchases and sales ledgers) and a trial balance. It is no good expecting the students to produce neat and tidy work if you do not set a good example on the board. Ideally more than one board should be available.

If you have your own classroom, it may even be possible to arrange for the boards to have permanent rulings for ledger, journal and cash book. If this is not possible an OHP transparency may be prepared for each of the rulings. When moving between classrooms, I always find it useful to carry my own set of felt pens or chalk, board rubber and board ruler – invariably you find there is no chalk, or the felt pens have run dry or have vanished.

Resources available

Check what resources are available. Some schools have sets of textbooks which are loaned out to the students for the school year; in other schools students are expected to purchase their own books.

In the former situation, it is sensible to check what books are available (bearing in mind the requirements of other Accounting teachers as well). Are there enough books to go round? Will each student be able to take home a copy of the textbook? School budgets are not bottomless pits, and you may have to make use of the books available rather than use a book of your choice.

Where students are required to purchase their own textbooks, cost may again be an important factor in the choice of books. This is invariably the case in further education where the cost, as well as the content, of possible textbooks has to be considered by the teacher.

It is important that students use correct accounting paper from the beginning of their course. This gets them into the habit of setting out accounting statements neatly and tidily. The use of this stationery can be dispensed with when the students progress to higher levels, but I think it is essential to introduce them to accounting paper when they first start their studies.

Once again, it is necessary to consider the availability of this stationery, and whether this is supplied by the school, or purchased by the students. Both exercise books and loose leaf paper are usually available – loose leaf paper is probably best as the answers to exercises can then be filed in chronological order, with a copy of a relevant handout if necessary.

Teacher activity 2.1 (for new teachers or teachers new to a school)

Check and/or find out:
- What resources such as overhead projectors are available in your school or department?
- Are facilities available for PowerPoint® presentations?
- Is there a system of reserving the equipment and how do you get it to your classroom?
- What textbooks, and how many, are available?
- What are the arrangements for students to obtain accounting stationery?
- Does each Accounting teacher prepare their own handouts and material, or is there a central bank?
- What facilities are available for teachers to prepare handouts?

Planning ahead
Obtain a copy of the syllabus
Once you are given your teaching timetable, it is essential that you obtain a copy of the syllabus for the courses you are to teach. (See Appendix B for addresses.) Check carefully that it is the syllabus relating to the year in which your students will sit the examination.

Plan a scheme of work
Draft a scheme of work. Decide in what order you will teach the syllabus, and plan how it will be spread over the school year (or two years if it is a two-year course). We will consider this in more detail later in this chapter.

Before the term actually starts it is sensible, if possible, to have lessons prepared for each class for the first few weeks. It is impossible to prepare detailed lessons for the whole year for every class you teach – but do have plans for the first few weeks. Remember, the first lesson will possibly be the first contact you have with that particular class. Even though they are probably only teenagers, your first few lessons will often influence their confidence in you as a teacher and in your knowledge of the subject.

In larger schools, it can happen that several classes are all following the same syllabus, but with different teachers. In this situation it is essential that the teachers decide on the order in which the topics are to be taught and how the syllabus will be spread over the school year. I have worked in a large college where there were six classes all following the same syllabus. The teachers decided on a scheme of work and how it would be broken down week by week. Common textbooks and handouts were used. In this way students who transferred from one class to another found their new group was at exactly the same point in the teaching programme.

Prepare lessons
Consider the objective of the lesson and how you can best achieve this – what do you want the students to know or to be able to do by the end of the session?

I have found that it is far better to start from the known and gradually work towards the unknown. In other words, when introducing a new topic refer back to earlier work that can be linked to the new material.

Every lesson cannot possibly be a 'perfect' lesson. You cannot plan every lesson you teach in the week down to the last detail. Remember that all the effort should not just come from you: the students must also put some effort into the lesson.

Students often like lessons to follow a routine, but it is vital that you vary the pace of teaching and the activities within the lesson. Do not let the lessons become so routine that the students get bored! The accepted method of teaching accounts used to be for the teacher to simply lecture the students on the appropriate topic and demonstrate the accounting principles involved by working an example on the board. All teachers will realise that students learn much better if they are involved in the lesson in some way.

You will soon get to know your students, and you can use this knowledge to plan how the various activities could be best used with that particular group. The lesson may consist of some teacher-led learning, some question–answer sessions, and some individual or group work. The students will soon get to know you and your style of teaching and recognise the different activities.

You should also try to ensure that you allow time to talk to individual students. Be approachable – don't stay behind your desk all the time! Talking to your students individually is invaluable. Where possible try to remain in the classroom when the students are leaving; some may prefer to have a word with you in private, rather than with the whole class listening.

We will consider lesson planning in Chapter 4.

Resources for students
Textbooks
Most examining boards publish a list of recommended textbooks. Do enquire whether such a list is available and obtain a copy. There is often an endorsed textbook on this list. This will have been written specifically to that particular syllabus and contain relevant examples and exercises.

You will find a list of useful textbooks in Appendix A.

Whilst it is often easy to use the same textbook year in and year out, try to break the mould and experiment with other books: you may find one that is more appropriate for the course you are teaching.

Teacher activity 2.2

Obtain a list of the recommended textbooks for the course on which you are to teach.
- Are you familiar with all the titles on the list?
- If there are titles that are not familiar to you, obtain a copy (some publishers are happy to supply inspection copies).
- Compare the contents of the books and the different ways topics are introduced.
- Consider recommending one of the books for use by students if school (or students' own) funds permit.
- Consider asking whether some of the books can be purchased for the school library, or for teachers' reference copies.

We have already mentioned that the choice of book may be determined by the sets of books already available in the school, and by the cost of books. Sometimes it is not possible for students to have an individual copy of the textbook, and in some cases textbooks are not available at all.

Handouts

Whatever textbook you choose, it will probably not contain enough material to keep your class busy all year. There is a limit to how many exercises a textbook can contain, so it will probably be necessary to produce handouts.

Don't attempt to produce all your handouts at once. You will gradually build up a stock of handouts which you can use in future years. Having taught for many years, I have a vast number of handouts. Even if a particular handout is not entirely suitable for a new syllabus, it can often be adapted relatively easily.

Where there are several teachers of the subject, it may be possible to compile a general file of graduated questions. I have taught in a college where this system operates very successfully, as everyone is willing to make contributions to the file.

Sometimes you will find that the class appreciate a set of notes on a particular topic, or a list of numbered points on how to deal with a certain set of entries.

If you plan to use handouts, do make sure that your students have a suitable file in which to store them.

PowerPoint presentations and the use of overhead projectors

I have found these can be very useful to illustrate the different stages that are necessary to produce various accounting statements. When teaching the topic of bank reconciliation, for example, it is meaningless to simply show the adjusted cash book and the reconciliation statement. A series of transparencies of the various stages is much more meaningful.

Once again, don't attempt to prepare all the presentations during your first year of teaching. Add to your 'library' gradually. Do not be tempted to have too much 'animation' in your presentation as this could actually detract from the subject matter!

Wall charts and posters

Make use of any display boards in the classroom. However, suitable wall charts and posters are not always easy to obtain and it may be easier to produce them yourself. Once again, do not try to produce them all at once.

It is not necessary to produce elaborate displays. The simple ones are often the best. Try to use wall charts to reinforce the topics you have covered in class. A very simple one may be simply a series of questions, for example:

> **Fixed assets**
>
> - Can you define fixed assets?
> - Can you name four fixed assets?
> - Can you list those fixed assets in correct Balance Sheet order?

Keep changing the displays – if you leave them there all term, the students will stop looking at them.

> **Teacher activity 2.3**
>
> - Design a simple wall chart listing the main terms used in connection with Balance Sheets.
> - Design a more complicated wall chart to illustrate how journals are written up from business documents.

Newspapers and periodicals

Students often think that accounting is just theoretical and does not actually happen in real life. It is important to take every opportunity to show that this is completely untrue.

Try to make use of anything in newspapers and periodicals to highlight that what they are learning in the classroom does actually happen in the *real* world. Articles in local newspapers about businesses that are known to the students will usually have far more impact than articles in the financial press.

If an article appears when the topic is actually being taught, all the better. Even if the topic was taught a few months previously, it will serve to reinforce that topic (and can obviously be used for next year's class).

Articles in the local newspaper about the bankruptcy or the cash flow problems of a local business can be cut out and either put on the display board or used as part of a handout. Even advertisements can be useful. For instance, an advertisement for a discount factor can be used when discussing ways to obtain repayment of debts quickly. Keep a lookout for anything that might help to bring the subject to life.

Films and videos

Films and videos are sometimes available for hire from educational bodies. It is worth checking the catalogue to see if there is anything suitable. Before showing the film to the class, it is a good idea to watch it first and prepare some activity for the students to complete after they have seen the film. It helps too if you decide to stop the film at specific points to check understanding, discuss a point or conduct a related activity.

Films can add variety to the presentation of the topic, but use them in moderation, not as an excuse for an 'easy' lesson!

Guest speakers

A short talk by a local business person or someone who works in the accounts department of a local organisation can help students understand the practical implications of accounting. When arranging such a visit, make sure that the speaker is aware of the level which the students have reached in their studies. Little benefit will be gained if the talk is pitched at too high a level.

Former students have often visited me during term time. As well as catching up with their personal news, I have often taken advantage of their visit by allowing them to chat informally with the present students about higher education and career opportunities.

Resources for teachers
Colleagues

Watching colleagues in action can be one of the most effective forms of professional development. If possible, arrange to sit in on the class of one of your colleagues and allow them to sit in on one of your classes. This can be helpful to both of you – provided it is carried out in the right spirit.

In larger schools it can happen that a large group of students is divided into two or more classes. Where these classes have the Accounting lesson at the same time, it may be possible to join them together for some lessons and share the teacher-led learning among all the teachers. I would not advise that this practice is followed for every lesson, but it can work very effectively if used on a few occasions during the school year.

Teacher activity 2.4

Think about, and also discuss with your colleagues, the following:
- Would it be possible to arrange to sit in on each other's classes?
- Would it be possible to arrange to 'shadow' a class of students to see their reactions to different teaching methods?
- Would it be possible to have regular meetings for subject teachers to exchange ideas etc?

The world of business

We must always bear in mind that our students may not have any experience of the world of work, so we must strive to bring the theoretical aspects of the subject to life. In an ideal scenario, the teacher will have experience of the business world as well as of the teaching profession. Unfortunately this is not always the case, and the teachers themselves may only know the theoretical aspects of accounting. If this applies to you, why not consider trying to gain some practical experience? This could be anything from taking a temporary job during the school holidays to asking a local business if you could 'shadow' a member of staff for a day or a week.

Textbooks

In addition to a list of books suitable for students, most examination boards publish a list of textbooks which are useful as teachers' reference books. Hopefully, you will also have a selection of personal textbooks which you can use for reference.

Published mark schemes and examiners' reports on examinations

We will consider these again in Chapter 6. Most examination boards publish a marking scheme and a report on each examination paper. Do try to obtain a copy. These are invaluable for seeing exactly how marks are awarded and explanations of where candidates lost marks.

Online resources

University of Cambridge International Examinations (CIE) have some useful websites for teachers. The main website, www.cie.org.uk, gives details about CIE, news and events (such as teacher training events and conferences), syllabuses for all the examinations, and so on. It has a site search feature, making it easy to find your way around.

In addition, the CIE Teacher Support Site provides access to past question papers, mark schemes and examiner reports. A scheme of work for each subject is gradually being added to the site. This breaks down the syllabus into teaching units, provides suggested teaching activities and recommends resources.

Teachers can also join the online subject discussion group. This is based on email technology, whereby an email sent by a member of the group is distributed automatically to all the other members of the group. This allows teachers throughout the world to exchange views on resources, teaching methods and so on; it can be likened to a global staffroom. The accounting group is very active and covers a wide range of topics, such as an enquiry from a teacher new to IGCSE Accounting asking other teachers which textbooks and resources they would recommend, a debate about the correct treatment of bad debts recovered in final accounts, a long discussion about the application of the realisation principle, as well as messages and responses about a wide range of other issues. Even the most experienced teachers may sometimes have doubts and queries. Asking other teachers may not only resolve the problem, but can show that many other teachers are also concerned about the same matter.

There are, of course, other websites which may be a useful source of material for teachers. The educational websites provided by the BBC and other institutions and companies such as the Financial Times also offer a useful source of background information and suggestions for exercises and assignments.

You will find a list of useful websites in Appendix B.

Professional publications

All the professional bodies produce regular magazines and newsletters for their members. Even if you are not a member, these are often available at local reference libraries. Such publications provide the latest information about accounting standards, which are probably not yet available in textbooks. Some information is also available on the websites of these professional bodies (see Appendix B).

Assessing your performance

We will concentrate on the assessment of students in Chapter 5. As well as assessing the students' performance, it is also important to assess your own performance.

You will probably be required to maintain a general record of the topic(s) covered in each lesson and any assignments set. Take this a step further, and keep your own more detailed notes. Add any comments about how the lesson was received by the students, whether it met the desired objectives, and the ways in which it could be improved. Make a note of any matters the students raised which you had not anticipated, or anything you omitted to include which, with hindsight, could have been included. To reduce the time and effort involved, I have always kept a single sheet for each of my classes with boxes for the appropriate comments. The objectives of each lesson can be completed when the lesson is being planned and the comments about whether these were achieved and any other remarks can be added afterwards. An example of a lesson record sheet is shown on page 12. Such detailed notes will be invaluable when planning to deliver a similar lesson in future.

More importantly, assessing your own work will help you to become a better teacher.

Example of a lesson record sheet

Year 2004 **Course title** IGCSE Accounting

Class 5B **Course duration** 30 weeks **Lessons per week** 2 × 1½ hours

Date	Objective	Achieved	Remarks	Homework
14/1/04	Introduction to the course. Introduction to accounts, Balance Sheet terms and preparation of simple Balance Sheet	Some time lost registering late arrivals, distributing books and stationery. All students prepared a very simple Balance Sheet.	Could improve handout of definitions by simply giving headings and allowing students to 'fill in' the actual definitions. Consider using in conjunction with OHP.	None given
17/1/04	More advanced Balance Sheets with division into different types of assets and liabilities	All students can give examples of fixed and current assets, long term and current liabilities. All completed two tasks.	A few new students joined the class. The re-cap of last lesson for the rest served as quick introduction for these students.	Assignment 1 (to be handed in next week)

12 Practical considerations

> **Teacher activity 2.5**
>
> Think about a lesson you have given. Draft a lesson record sheet, or use the example provided, and make notes on the following:
> - What was the main objective of the lesson?
> - Did you achieve the results you anticipated?
> - Did the class react in the way you anticipated?
> - Did you complete all you expected to accomplish?
> - Could the lesson presentation have been improved?
> - Could you have used more appropriate examples?

Interpreting the syllabus
Assessment aims

Most examination syllabuses set out the assessment aims and objectives. These are intended to provide guidance for teachers. Take time to study these and decide exactly what is expected from your students. You will sometimes find that these aims and objectives are couched in language with which you are not familiar. Don't worry if at first you are puzzled by these – many teachers experience a slight sense of anxiety on first reading these sections of a syllabus.

Take each aim and objective separately and study the information provided. You could even make your own list of how that information translates into the various accounting skills. If you are a new teacher, or new to a particular syllabus, don't be afraid to ask colleagues for help – everyone has to start somewhere. There may be other teachers at the school who are teaching the same course, or have taught it in the past. Whilst some teachers might not be happy to share their handouts, they are usually prepared to discuss their teaching strategies and the application of the syllabus.

The aims of the IGCSE Accounting syllabus can be summarised as:
- To help students understand the ways in which accounting provides useful information for individuals, businesses, non-trading organisations and the general public.
- To help students understand the basic principles, procedures and common terminology used in accounting.
- To help students understand the aims and activities of businesses and non-trading organisations and the ways in which accounting can assist in the achievement and recording of these.
- To help students develop numerical, literary, communicative, interpretive and presentation skills.
- To help students develop skills in accuracy, orderliness and logical thought.

The aims of other Accounting syllabuses follow a similar pattern.

> **Teacher activity 2.6**
> - Consider each of the aims of the syllabus separately.
> - Think how each of the aims can be achieved through the teaching of Accounting.
> - Think how each of the aims can be related to the main topic areas of the syllabus.

Assessment objectives

The IGCSE Accounting syllabus lists three assessment objectives (or skills) which are:
- Knowledge with understanding
- Analysis
- Evaluation

The first section requires that examination candidates know and understand the basic facts, terms and principles of the topics on the syllabus. Candidates need to be able to demonstrate this knowledge by answering questions involving both language and numerical skills. In practical terms, this assessment objective covers questions involving definition of accounting terms, explanation of accounting principles and the application of basic double entry principles.

The assessment objective of analysis requires examination candidates to be able to select appropriate accounting data, and present this in appropriate accounting form. In practical terms, this assessment objective covers questions involving the preparation of final accounts, correction of errors and suspense accounts, and similar topics. In these topics the candidate is required to apply the knowledge to a particular circumstance, not recall information learned by rote.

The last assessment objective of evaluation requires examination candidates to be able to evaluate and interpret accounting information and to draw reasoned conclusions. In practical terms, this assessment objective covers questions involving the calculation and interpretation of accounting ratios, profit correction and other areas where candidates are required to explain the effects of a given problem, or to suggest appropriate courses of action in a given situation.

The assessment objectives of other Accounting syllabuses follow a similar pattern.

Teacher activity 2.7

Consider the following topics. Can you identify which of the three assessment objectives (skills) of the IGCSE syllabus is being tested in each case?
- Explaining the entries in a ledger account
- Preparing a Manufacturing Account
- Writing up a three-column cash book
- Explaining the dangers of a shortage of working capital
- Preparing a Balance Sheet of a non-trading organisation
- Suggesting how a trader may reduce the risk of bad debts

The answers are in Appendix E.

Teacher activity 2.8

Consider the following IGCSE examination question.

Carol Crespo's business is divided into two departments – Department A and Department B.

The following information is provided for the year ended 31 March 2002.

	Department A	Department B
	$	$
Stock 1 April 2001	1 100	3 900
Stock 31 March 2002	800	4 800
Sales	22 000	66 400
Purchases	12 300	43 200
Returns inwards	–	400
Carriage inwards	200	–

a) Prepare a columnar Trading Account for Carol Crespo for the year ended 31 March 2002 to show the gross profit earned by each department. Total columns are not required.

b) State two reasons why it is useful for Carol to know the results of each department of the business.

> After comparing the gross profit of each department, Carol is disappointed with the results of Department A and is considering closing the department.
>
> c) Explain why it would be more meaningful to compare the percentage of gross profit to sales of each department.
>
> d) Explain **two non-financial** factors which Carol should consider before closing the department.
>
> *This question tests more than one assessment objective (skill). Can you identify which objective is being tested in each section of the question?*
>
> *The answer is in Appendix E.*

Each syllabus usually contains a specification grid which shows the relationship between the assessment objectives (skills) and the scheme of assessment. This grid shows the approximate weighting of the assessment objectives to give an indication of their relative importance. For example, each paper on the IGCSE Accounting syllabus places a greater emphasis on the skill of knowledge with understanding than on either of the other two skills. Compare this with the GCE O level Accounting syllabus Paper 2, where there is a greater emphasis on the skill of analysis.

> **Teacher activity 2.9**
>
> Study the questions on a past examination paper (excluding multiple-choice) and analyse them between the different assessment objectives (skills).
>
> You should find that they approximate with the percentages given in the specification grid for that particular syllabus.
>
> Remember that one question may include elements of all the assessment objectives.

Converting the syllabus into a scheme of work

The order in which the syllabus is set out is not intended to show the order in which the topics should be taught. It is up to the teacher to decide the order that best suits their style of teaching. However, where several teachers are all teaching the same syllabus, a joint decision needs to be made on the order in which the topics will be taught.

To a certain extent the order of the topics may also depend on which textbook is being used. Some textbooks cover accruals and prepayments before depreciation; other cover these topics in reverse order. This may influence the order in which the topics are taught. The endorsed textbook for IGCSE Accounting covers them in the order listed below.

Suggested scheme of work for IGCSE Accounting
- Outline of basic purpose of accounting. Balance Sheet equation: preparation of a simple Balance Sheet
- Double entry book-keeping: two- and three-column cash books
- Trial balance: errors not affecting the trial balance
- Petty cash books
- Business documents and books of prime entry
- Elementary final accounts
- Accounting principles
- Accruals and prepayments in the ledger and in final accounts
- Depreciation of fixed assets in the ledger and in final accounts: disposal of fixed assets
- Bad debts and provision for doubtful debts in the ledger and in final accounts
- Bank reconciliation statements
- Journal entries and the correction of errors
- Control accounts
- Incomplete records
- Accounts of clubs and societies
- Partnership accounts
- Manufacturing Accounts
- Departmental Accounts
- Analysis and interpretation

Most of the topics involve more than one of the assessment objectives (or skills). The very first topic of introduction to Accounting and introduction to Balance Sheets will primarily be an application of the objective of knowledge with understanding. Once the students are actually preparing Balance Sheets, the second objective of analysis is being applied. Similarly, basic journal entries primarily involve the skill of knowledge with understanding, but more complex entries involving the correction of errors introduce the second objective of analysis.

Evaluation often has to be left until later in the course when the students have enough knowledge about the subject to be able to apply that knowledge to given situations. It is, however, important to try to introduce elementary evaluation exercises into lessons as early as possible. Students must be encouraged to think about the effects and implications of the accounting statements they have prepared. For example, when preparing a set of final accounts in which the Balance Sheet reveals a shortage of working capital, I take the opportunity to draw from the students the ways in which this situation could be remedied.

Similarly, if final accounts for two different businesses are prepared in consecutive lessons, students could do a simple comparison. Even if ratio analysis has not been formally introduced, students are usually able to make useful comments if given suitable prompting.

What topic to start with

Try to make sure that the students actually prepare some kind of accounting statement in the first lesson – however elementary that statement may be. Students like to think that they have actually done some accounts in the first lesson. Listening to a lot of theory in the first lesson will only create boredom and will often be meaningless to them at this stage. It is obviously necessary to explain some accounting terms in the first lesson, but it is important to keep the explanations to a minimum and intersperse them with activities.

Ideally, I would always begin an introduction to an accounting course with the basic principles of double entry. However, you will see from the suggested scheme of work on page 17 that I now favour the Balance Sheet approach. The reason behind this is that during the first week of the school year the students are still settling down and sorting out options. It has often happened that, for various reasons, a new student has joined my class in week two. If a student is missing for the first week they can copy up any notes missed on basic definitions of assets, liabilities and so on, and complete some of the simple exercises undertaken in class. Any gaps in their understanding can be filled when we return to the topic of final accounts in a later lesson.

The principles of double entry are the basis of all accounting procedures. However, if a student is absent when double entry is first introduced they often struggle throughout the whole course, and I have found that using the Balance Sheet approach reduces this risk.

Teacher activity 2.10

Study the topics in the syllabus. List the topics in a suitable order for teaching.

Remember, this may be influenced by your choice of textbook.

Planning the year's work

Once you have decided the order in which you will teach the syllabus topics, the next task is to prepare a week-by-week breakdown. In order to complete this task you will have to consider:
- Is the course taught over one or two years?
- How many weeks are there in the school year?
- On what dates are the examinations to be taken?
- How many lessons are there each week in the subject?
- Are all the lessons the same length?
- How much time are you going to allow for revision?

Do also remember to allow for unexpected events which cause class time to be lost. No one can predict that the school will be closed for a week because of flooding, or how much time will be lost because of fire evacuation practice, for example. You may even be ill and unable to teach your classes for a few days or weeks.

Preparing a detailed scheme of work

I usually prepare a chart ruled up for the number of available weeks, showing the holiday periods and the examination dates. I then indicate a period of, say, two weeks at the end of the course for revision, and leave at least one other week 'blank' as a safety measure for any emergencies.

The next step is to spread the topics over the available weeks. Some topics such as petty cash books can usually be taught within one lesson; other topics such as double entry will need to be spread over several lessons, adding a little more detail each time. With experience you will learn how much time, on average, is required for each topic. Don't be afraid to compare notes with your colleagues and teachers who have taught that particular course.

You may find that under the original plan you would be starting a new topic, which requires more than one week, just before the school closes for a holiday. This is obviously not a good course of action, so switch topics around. In the suggested scheme of work, there is no reason at all why small topics such as petty cash books, bank reconciliation and accounting principles cannot be moved into more convenient 'slots'.

In addition to providing your students with a copy of the syllabus, it is often useful to provide them with a programme outlining the scheme of work. At its simplest this may list the main topics in the order they will be taught. A more detailed programme may include a week-by-week breakdown of the topics, textbook references, weeks when homework or an assignment will be set, and so on.

Teacher activity 2.11

Using the list you prepared in activity 2.10, prepare a week-by-week breakdown of the topics.

Remember to leave time for revision and for unexpected events.

LOOKING BACK

Careful planning and preparation are important if successful lessons are to be delivered.

At the beginning of the school year:
- Did you consider the facilities and resources available?
- Did you consider the aims and objectives of the syllabus?
- Did you convert the syllabus into a detailed scheme of work?

Retrospective assessment of the suitability of the plans and the effectiveness of lessons allow improvements to be made for the future.

At the end of the course, or the end of the term:
- Did you assess your own performance as well as that of the students?

3 The role of skills in Accounting

This chapter concentrates on the skills students of Accounting need to acquire. Some of these skills are specific to the subject, and others are related to the learning process in general.

These skills may be summarised as:
- practical skills
- numerical skills
- language skills
- learning skills
- reasoning skills
- integrating skills.

Practical skills

These are obviously specific to the subject and are the particular skills we want our students to acquire when preparing written accounting statements.

Firstly, it is important that students learn to prepare their accounting statements in a neat and tidy manner. This reduces the chance of mistakes being made. We have already referred to the importance of using accounting stationery when beginning a course in Accounting. Remember, you need to practise what you preach and make sure that your work on the board, on slides and on handouts is neat and tidy.

Students do need to be taught to list columns of figures so that the units are in alignment, the tens are in alignment, and so on. This may be obvious to us, as teachers, but we cannot expect the students to know unless they have learned this in mathematics lessons, or unless we tell them.

Similarly, we cannot expect our students to draw total lines with the aid of a ruler unless they are taught to do this. Where it is necessary to draw up accounts (on examination papers, or when preparing petty cash books, for example), insist that the columns are drawn using a ruler, not freehand.

We must recognise that sometimes students write something down and then realise they have made a mistake. It is important to teach them to cross the incorrect items out neatly, and write the amended item above, or alongside. Similarly, we must discourage students from changing a figure by writing a second figure over it.

Sometimes the marking scheme for an examination question allows one or two marks for presentation. Candidates are likely to forfeit such marks if their work is untidy and the words and figures are unclear. Consider the following answer by a student asked to prepare a ledger account from given data.

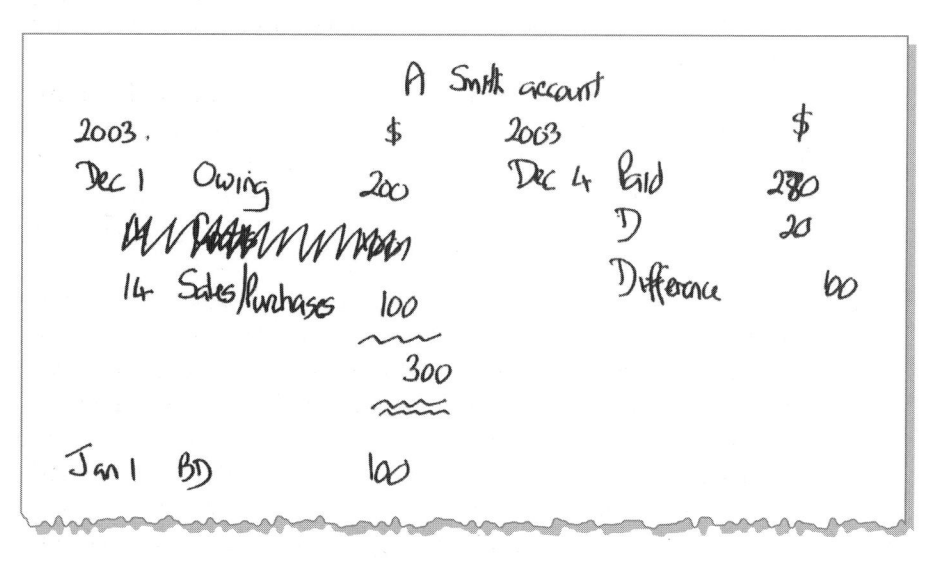

[Handwritten ledger account:]

A Smith account

2003.		$	2003		$
Dec 1	Owing	200	Dec 4	Paid	280
~~(scribbled out)~~				D	20
14	~~Sales~~/Purchases	100		Difference	60
		300			
Jan 1	B/D	100			

You should be able to count at least 12 presentation errors. Refer to the end of the chapter if you have not been able to spot them all.

Teacher activity 3.1

Compose an account or an accounting statement, or reproduce a piece of work prepared by a student (remove the name of the student!) which contains a number of errors of presentation.

Present this to the class and ask them if they can find a given number of the errors, and why a student would probably lose marks for the piece of work.

You could copy this onto a transparency and display it using an overhead projector.

Numerical skills

I would be quite wealthy if I had a dollar for every time a student has said to me, 'I'm not very good at Maths, so I won't be able to do accounts'. I am sure you have similar things said to you. Emphasise to your students that this is not necessarily the case. Whilst some elementary numerical skills are required, accounting involves many other abilities such as a methodical and logical approach to accounting problems.

Obviously, the ability to do simple addition and subtraction is necessary. Students should have already learned to do this in their Mathematics classes. They will also need to be able to calculate simple percentages and ratios in accounting, but, again, the students should already know how to do these calculations.

The use of calculators is usually permitted in Accounting examinations. Ensure that your students know how to carry out basic arithmetic calculations on their calculator. Students will probably be able to use calculators but do check that they are making the best use of them. It is not unknown for students to be unsure how to use the percentage key, for example.

It is useful to train students not to place absolute reliance on their calculator. Some think that whatever figure the calculator shows it must be correct. They do not seem to realise that there may have been an error on the part of the operator! I always encourage students to estimate the answer to a calculation before entering the numbers into the calculator.

I used to assume that students were familiar with basic mental arithmetic – but soon realised that many are absolutely reliant on their calculators. I now encourage students to perform simple calculations without reference to their calculators. Elementary percentages such as 10%, 5% and $2\frac{1}{2}$% often occur in accounting questions. When any percentages occur in an accounting exercise for the first time, I always ensure that students know how to calculate a simple percentage quickly, without using a calculator.

Teacher activity 3.2

Check that your students know a quick and easy way to calculate the following percentages of a given figure, without using a calculator:
- $33\frac{1}{3}$%
- 20%
- 5%
- $2\frac{1}{2}$%

Language skills

There are necessarily some technical words that students need to learn. Remember that words which we, as teachers of Accounting, take for granted will not be familiar to your students. Every time a new technical word or phrase arises, you should explain it to your students. Don't assume that they can work out the meaning for themselves. It may be possible to ask the class leading questions, and actually build up a definition of the word from the responses you receive.

I always encourage students to maintain a list of technical words and add to that list each time a new word is introduced. If you do this, make sure that:
- the students have a suitable notebook or folder for the purpose;
- time is allowed in the class for students to record the information;
- students write down the correct spelling of the word;
- students write down a full and correct definition.

In subsequent lessons I make sure that I use these words and phrases to check whether the students have remembered them. If the students seem doubtful they can refer back to their notebooks and revise the meaning of that particular word.

Whilst Accounting examinations consist mostly of numerical work, some questions may require students to produce a written statement. These may begin 'Explain …', 'Describe …', 'Comment on …', 'Discuss …' and so on. In Accounting examinations, grammatical errors are not usually penalised, but examiners must be able to understand what the student is trying to describe.

We all know that students much prefer to be 'doing' accounts rather than writing about them, but it is important to train students to attempt written answers from an early stage in their studies. I usually start by giving students words to define, progress to short explanations, and gradually build up until they are able to attempt more sophisticated paragraphs commenting on figures or discussing courses of action.

Obviously, the vast majority of work set for students will be numerical. Try to include a short written answer on as many assessments as possible to give your students practice at written work.

Whenever you are talking about accounting with your students, whether it is a question and answer session or whether it is discussing homework with an individual student, do insist that they use the correct technical terms. That way they will become more familiar with the meaning of the words and phrases.

Asking a class the question 'On which side of the account should this be recorded?' often results in the answer 'On the right-hand side' in the first few lessons on double entry. My automatic response to this is 'I only have a debit hand and a credit hand – not a right and left!' Whilst this causes amusement, I do get a correct answer when I pose similar questions later. Similarly, on another basic topic, do discourage your students from referring to the debit side and credit side of a Balance Sheet.

Teacher activity 3.3

Go through the syllabus and make a list of any technical words and phrases which the students will need to learn. Write a short definition of each word or phrase which will be suitable for your students.

Introduce the students to these technical words and phrases gradually. Make sure that the students maintain a list of these words and phrases with suitable definitions, and encourage them to add to the list each time a 'new' word is introduced.

Learning skills

Whilst much of the classroom learning will be teacher-led, it is important to encourage the students to learn for themselves. By learning how to study, students will develop a skill which will be invaluable in all future learning situations – in school, or in further or higher education.

We have already discussed encouraging students to maintain a notebook of definitions of technical words or phrases. If on a future occasion students are doubtful of the meaning of a technical word, they will be able to refer to their own notes.

The teacher cannot possibly be at the beck and call of every individual student in the class to answer simple factual questions. Students must be encouraged to act on their own initiative. Make sure that they are familiar with the list of contents and the index in their textbook.

Obviously, we want our students to understand the principles underlying the accounting statements they are preparing. Sometimes, however, we have to accept that they will need to learn things by rote. (The list of errors not revealed by a trial balance is something that immediately springs to mind.) The use of mnemonics may be helpful in this context. A mnemonic can be in the form of a phrase, a group of letters or a group of symbols which help the students recall a piece of information. If you encourage students to compose their own mnemonics, they are more likely to remember them.

Many teachers will be familiar with

```
            |
            |
   P  E  A  |  R  L  S
            |
            |
```

in connection with the debit and credit items in a trial balance, and with

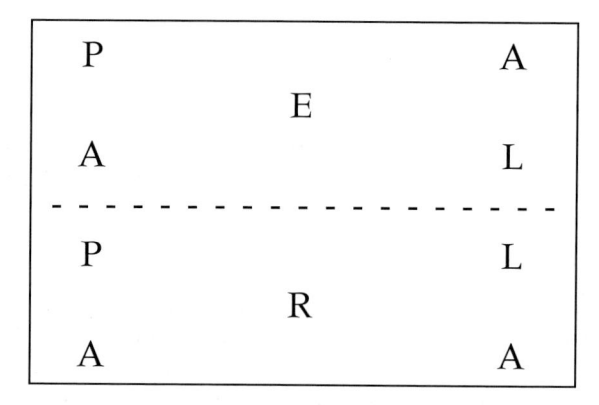

```
   P                    A
            E
   A                    L
   - - - - - - - - - - - -
   P                    L
            R
   A                    A
```

in connection with accrued and prepaid expenses and revenue.
Please refer to the end of the chapter if you are not familiar with these.

> **Teacher activity 3.4**
>
> Compose a mnemonic which would be of help to your students.
>
> Make a note of any mnemonics your students compose or which you find in textbooks or other sources which may be of use to your students.

We have already mentioned the importance of trying to relate the studies in the classroom to the world of business. Students should be aware that accounting is not just a classroom activity – it is part of 'the world of work'. Discuss with them anything which appears on television or in the newspapers which they can relate to their studies. Encourage them to look at pages other than, say, sport or fashion.

Reasoning skills

Students need to be able to apply facts to a given situation and to come to a reasoned conclusion. These reasoning skills cannot be learned by rote; they can only be developed gradually over time as the student absorbs more factual information and becomes more familiar with the subject. This is a process which cannot be rushed – it must be encouraged and developed slowly.

Even in the first few weeks of their Accounting course, students can be given basic problems to solve by reasoning skills. Consider including the application of simple reasoning skills when teaching a two-column cash book.

Student activity 3.1

Draw on the students' basic knowledge of double entry and make the necessary entries for cash paid into bank. Using that as a basis, ask the students to suggest how the entries for cash withdrawn from the bank for office use will appear. They can usually work it out for themselves.

Student activity 3.2

Having made the necessary entries to record a cheque received from a debtor, ask the students to suggest the entries necessary to record a dishonoured cheque. (Obviously make sure that they understand the meaning of the term 'dishonoured'!) Once again, the students will usually be able to work it out for themselves.

More advanced reasoning skills will need to be introduced as students cover more complex matters in the syllabus. With the right prompting from the teacher, students are often able to apply logical reasoning to an accounting problem and arrive at a sensible conclusion.

Consider the calculation of the debtors' collection period and the creditors' payment period. Once students have been taught how to apply the appropriate ratios, they need to be made aware of the significance of these figures. Try to encourage them to think for themselves rather than giving them a list to memorise. I try to prepare a list of elementary questions to put to the class, which can be used to encourage their reasoning skills. I may ask such things as:
- What does it mean when the debtors' collection period is 40 days?
- What does it mean when the credit allowed is 30 days, but the collection period is 40 days?

- How will the business be affected if the debtors' collection period is 40 days and the creditors' payment period is 30 days?
- Has the business got enough money to be able to continue this policy?

The weaker students often find a simple diagram of the working capital cycle useful in trying to envisage the importance of working capital. I usually draw a circle representing working capital on the board. Students can often apply simple reasoning skills to questions about the effects of a pause at some point of the circle.

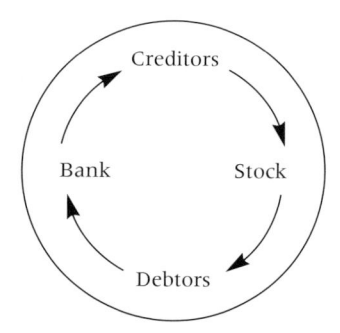

Teacher activity 3.5

On an overhead projector transparency, or on the board, prepare a simple working capital circle.

Make a list of a few situations, such as:

1 A large quantity of stock proves to be unsaleable.
2 A debtor owing a substantial amount of money is unable to pay his account.
3 A creditor states that goods ordered will not be delivered until three months after the promised date.

Ask the students to consider the effects (including the 'knock-on' effects) of each of the situations on each of the constituent elements of the working capital.

Integrating skills

We have already mentioned the importance of referring back to earlier work when introducing a new topic and linking each lesson to a previous one.

Try to take every opportunity to link a new topic with topics already covered. Not only does this act as a method of revising the earlier work, but it also helps students to appreciate that all the individual sections of the syllabus are connected and integrally linked together.

Introducing the topic of correcting errors by journal entries and the use of suspense accounts is an obvious place to revise the purpose of a trial balance and the errors not revealed by the trial balance. Introducing the topic of ratios and working capital is an obvious place to revise the definitions of current assets, current liabilities and working capital.

As well as relating one topic to another within the subject, it is important to try to establish a link with as many other subjects as possible. Some students seem to be under the misapprehension that each of their school subjects is 'complete' in itself, and there is absolutely no link between them. Mentioning that you have studied (or taught) other subjects is often met with astonishment.

Accounting is obviously closely linked with Mathematics, so try to work closely with Mathematics teachers. It is much easier if the students have covered such things as ratios in their Mathematics classes before you introduce them to the topic of ratio analysis.

There is also a strong link with Business Studies and Commerce. If your Accounting students are also following a Commerce course, there will no doubt be an overlap on such topics as business documents and banking. Try to liaise with the Commerce teacher. It would be extremely helpful, both for teachers and for students, if such a topic was covered in both subjects at the same time. The Commerce lesson could concentrate on the purpose of various business documents, and the Accounting lesson could concentrate on the use of those documents when writing up a set of accounting records. Similarly, the topic of banking on a Commerce syllabus could be linked to the topic of bank reconciliation on an Accounting syllabus. Where timetabling permits, it may even be possible to give a joint lesson. This is an ideal way of showing the students that the subjects should not be 'compartmentalised' but that they are integrally linked.

Assessments covering more than one subject are a practical way of demonstrating how the different subjects are linked to each other. Co-operation with teachers of other subjects is essential for both the setting and marking of such assessments.

You will find a simple 'cross-subject' assessment in Appendix C on pages 73–4.

Teacher activity 3.6

Construct a simple 'cross-subject' assessment, introducing at least two other subjects in addition to Accounting.

You will need to consult other teachers to establish which topics the students have covered.

Even where there is no 'obvious' link to another subject, it may be possible for the teachers to design some activity which could benefit more than one subject. If the students have lessons in keyboard skills, it may be possible to ask the teacher to allow them to type some business documents, which you could use for your lesson on that topic. If the students have Art lessons, it may be possible to ask the teacher to allow them to design some posters on Accounting.

It is not always feasible to arrange outside visits purely for Accounting purposes. Such visits are often easier to integrate in the Business Studies or Commerce syllabus. Try to find out if any such visits are arranged, and encourage your students to take the opportunity of seeing accounting activities in the 'real' world.

> **LOOKING BACK**
>
> Students of Accounting need to develop various skills. Consider the skills we have discussed in this chapter.
> - Do you try to include all these skills in your teaching?
> - Do you include other skills, not discussed in this chapter, in your teaching?
> - Do you teach these skills specifically, or are they simply implied in the lesson content?

Errors in the ledger account on page 22

1 'Owing' is not adequate for 'Balance'
2 An untidy scribbling
3 Figures out of alignment
4 'Sales/purchases' too imprecise
5 Total lines not straight
6 No '2004' above Jan 1
7 'BD' is not adequate for 'Balance b/d'
8 'Paid' is not adequate for 'Bank' (or 'Cash')
9 Figure over-written
10 'D' is not adequate for 'Discount'
11 'Difference' is not adequate for 'Balance c/d'
12 Closing balance undated
13 No total lines

Answers to mnemonics on page 26

P	E	A	R	L	S
u	x	s	e	i	a
r	p	s	v	a	l
c	e	e	e	b	e
h	n	t	n	i	s
a	s	s	u	l	
s	e	s	e	i	
e	s			t	
s				i	
				e	
				s	

Prepaid		Asset
	Expense	
Accrued		Liability

Prepaid		Liability
	Revenue	
Accrued		Asset

4 Teaching skills in Accounting

Once you have planned your scheme of work you need to convert this into a series of lessons. This will be determined to a large extent by the number of lessons per week and the length of each lesson. Sometimes one topic may have to be spread over one or more lessons; sometimes you may have to modify your scheme of work slightly so that you can introduce a new topic in the 45-minute lesson rather than in the 30-minute lesson.

An Accounting lesson should obviously include the basic elements of:
- referring to the principles covered in previous lessons;
- introducing the topic to be covered this lesson;
- demonstrating the application of the principles involved in the new topic;
- providing practical work for the students.

How the lesson is actually delivered obviously depends not only on the teacher's own personality and experience, but also on the particular topic. Some topics are necessarily based on teacher-led learning whilst others can be based on learning through activities.

In the 1950s and 1960s a typical Accounting lesson consisted of the teacher lecturing the students on a topic, demonstrating the accounting principles by working an exercise on the board (which the students copied down) and then the students completing a similar exercise on their own. Today's teachers have many more resources at their disposal and understand the need to get the students involved as much as possible in the lesson. We all appreciate the need to vary the lessons and incorporate as many different activities as possible. The number of students in the class and the facilities available will obviously influence the type of activities which are possible.

> **Teacher activity 4.1**
>
> Think about your classroom and consider what facilities it offers.
>
> Consider:
> - using an overhead projector or PowerPoint slides;
> - showing films and videos;
> - using the Internet;
> - moving the furniture to facilitate group work or role play.

Varying the format of lessons

We have already discussed the practice of varying the style and pace of lessons as much as possible. The format of the lesson will obviously depend on the topic being taught – in some cases we will be able to draw on the students' own knowledge and experience, but in other cases the lesson will have to be almost completely teacher-led.

Compare the following three lesson plans. The first involves the students in a very active role; the second is a blend of student-based activities and teacher-led learning; the third is based on teacher-led learning.

Lesson plan 1

Topic – Introduction to bank reconciliation statements

Aims	Understanding why the bank's records and those of the customer differ, reasons why bank reconciliation is necessary, updating cash books and preparing elementary bank reconciliation statements
Requirements	Large white or black board (preferably two boards) Chalk or felt pens Pre-prepared OHP transparency (see below) – or handouts if an OHP is not practicable
Brief introduction	Transactions affecting the trader's bank account need to be recorded by both the bank and the trader.

Select one student to act as the bank official and another student to act as the trader. These do not need to be the most able students (the rest of the class will be saying what entries are required). Ask each of the chosen students to stand by one of the boards with chalk/felt pen.

Refer the students to the OHP transparency, or handout. This should contain a list of dates and transactions such as:

2004
March
- 1   Hassan is a trader. According to both the cash book and the bank records he has $4000 in the bank.
- 4   Hassan gave Sara a cheque for $200.
- 8   The bank takes $200 from Hassan's bank account to pay Sara.
- 11   The bank paid $50 for an insurance premium direct to Hassan's insurance company.
- 13   Hassan received and banked a cheque for $100 from Abdul.
- 19   The bank discovers that Abdul has no funds in his bank account and that the cheque is dishonoured.
- 21   Hassan is notified by the bank that Abdul's cheque is dishonoured.
- 26   Hassan gave Mohammed a cheque for $350.
- 28   Hassan paid $660 cash sales into the bank.
- 30   The bank took $15 from Hassan's account for bank charges.

Work through the list of transactions, discussing each one with the students and asking them to tell the two students acting as 'writers' what entries should be made in each set of books. The trader's books will need to have a bank account and other accounts required in order to show the double entries. The bank's books can be limited to an account for the trader (Hassan) and an account for the stock of money. Obviously this is a very simplified version of the bank procedures, but it is adequate for this purpose.

(I find it useful to give the students who are the 'writers' a list of dates on which they should be making entries in their 'books' so they are not tempted to write when no entry is required – otherwise the whole purpose of the exercise is lost.)

The two accounts can be balanced, and will obviously show different figures.

The student acting as the bank official can now return to his/her seat.

Discuss with the students how the trader's records can be brought up to date. The student acting as the trader can make the necessary entries (with guidance from the other students) and the account can be re-balanced.

The student acting as the trader can now return to his/her place in the classroom.

Discuss the reasons why the balance shown by the revised cash book still does not agree with that shown by the bank. Prepare a bank reconciliation statement on the board.

Depending on the length of the lesson, the students can then be presented with a handout of a bank statement and a trader's cash book and asked to select items which cause the difference in the balances. An exercise of updating the cash book and preparing the bank reconciliation statement can follow – the teacher providing general guidance but allowing the students to make the necessary entries. (I check at regular points to make sure that everyone has made the correct entries, for example what items are debited in the cash book, what items are credited, what is new balance on the cash book, which items are added in the bank reconciliation statement, which are deducted).

I usually use a handout for the first exercise on this topic, as students sometimes 'spoil' the page of the textbook by putting a mass of ticks and crosses.

Lesson plan 2

Topic – Introduction to partnerships

Aims Understanding the advantages and disadvantages of partnership businesses, the role of the partnership agreement, and elementary profit appropriation

Requirements White or black board
Chalk or felt pens
Pre-prepared OHP transparency (see below) if desired

Brief introduction What constitutes a partnership business.

Students to divide into groups of 2 or 3. Each group to make the following lists:

1. Names of four partnership businesses known to them
2. Four advantages of being in a partnership rather than being a sole trader
3. Four disadvantages of being in a partnership rather than being a sole trader

Ask one member of each group to read out the names of the businesses the group has listed. These can be recorded on the board. There may be some overlap, but hopefully the final list will have a variety of businesses. It may be necessary to prompt the students to name other businesses in addition to those listed. Use the list to show the types of business where partnerships are quite common.

Follow a similar pattern with the advantages and disadvantages of partnerships. It may be necessary to rearrange the final list into a suitable order and with appropriate wording. Sometimes it is useful to have an OHP transparency with a pre-prepared list of the advantages and disadvantages which the students can then copy (or they can be given a handout instead).

Working in groups, students can be asked to list the things they think partners should agree before they actually start the partnership business. Following the previous pattern, each group's list is read out and an overall list built up on the board.

This then leads into a formal introduction to the accounting elements of a partnership agreement. Again, a pre-prepared OHP transparency can be used, or the items listed on the board, which the students can copy, or they can be given a handout.

A simple example of two partners, with different capitals and different workloads, can illustrate how interest on capital and drawings, and salaries, can be appropriate. (These can be based on two students in the group – I usually pick on the most unlikely partnership within the group!)

On the board, this can then be converted into an Appropriation Account in the correct format.

Depending on the length of the lesson, the students can then be asked to prepare an Appropriation Account from given data.

Lesson plan 3

Topic – Introduction to depreciation of fixed assets

Aims Understanding why most fixed assets lose value over time and the main methods of depreciation

Requirements White or black board
Chalk or felt pens
Pre-prepared OHP transparency (see below) if desired

Ask the students the following question: 'My car is now three years old. I haven't had any accidents, but why isn't it worth what I paid for it?'

Draw from the students the fact that it has depreciated. Give a definition of the term *depreciation*.

On the board, compile a list of causes of depreciation (on fixed assets generally, not just the car). The list may need re-arranging into a suitable order, or a pre-prepared OHP transparency can be used. The students can be allowed time to write these down, or be given a handout.

Take the opportunity to stress that depreciation does not involve the outflow of money. If a student raises the fact that some assets appreciate, take the opportunity to briefly explain this (without going into too much detail as this is not on the IGCSE or O level syllabus).

Write a short extract from a trader's Balance Sheet on the board (using the date of the lesson), showing a few fixed assets at cost price and the dates of purchase. Again, a pre-prepared OHP transparency can be used. Ask the students why the Balance Sheet is misleading.

Draw from the students the fact that these assets will have depreciated. Prompt the students about the application of the principles of matching and prudence. Revise as necessary.

Describe the differences between the three main methods of depreciation – *straight line, diminishing balance* and *revaluation*. Prompt the students to state when each type of depreciation may be used.

Using a simple example written on the board, or on a pre-prepared handout, or on a pre-prepared OHP transparency, show the calculation of these methods of depreciation (for, say, two years). Allow time for students to write down these calculations.

Depending on the length of the lesson, students can then be asked to prepare similar calculations using a simple example from a handout or textbook.

> **Teacher activity 4.2**
>
> Plan a lesson on the introduction of a new partner (if following the IGCSE syllabus) or purchase of a business (if following the O level syllabus).
>
> Ensure that the students play an active part in the lesson. This could involve group work considering the advantages and disadvantages of the proposal, reasons why goodwill is payable etc.
>
> Role play could also be introduced (one student acting as a potential partner and other students as the existing partners, or one student acting as the person selling the business and another student as the potential purchaser).
>
> Advertisements for local businesses for sale can be utilised.
>
> Teacher-led learning will be necessary to demonstrate the necessary entries in the books of account.

Providing a complete picture

The difference between fixed and current assets should be explained early in the course. Weeks later when a Balance Sheet is being prepared in class, take the opportunity to revise the meaning of these terms: students may well remember which of the assets should be listed under fixed and which under current, but are they able to actually define the terms fixed and current assets? Linking of previous topics to those currently being taught is essential for students to see the complete picture and also serves to refresh their memories of topics taught several weeks ago.

Because of the limited number of pages, most textbooks contain assignments based on one topic only. For example,

- exercises involving two- or three-column cash books do not require double entries into the ledger;
- exercises involving the preparation of final accounts do not require the transfers from ledger accounts.

Examination questions are necessarily in a similar format – it is just not possible, or practical, to ask candidates to produce a full set of accounts.

It is important that students realise how all these sections fit together. Occasionally it is quite useful to work through a complete set of accounts – from the opening journal entry, through the day-to-day transactions to the trial balance, the closing of the ledger accounts as appropriate, and the final accounts. A long exercise such as this must be completed over several lessons, and in sections with the students checking their work at the end of each section. Students must also be made aware of the reasons for completing such an exercise and that examination papers will not contain questions of this length.

Some aspects of how various accounting procedures are linked together are often overlooked, or are mentioned only once. The closing of ledger accounts is an example. We teach our students to balance the cash book and the personal accounts, but often overlook what happens to the rest of the accounts at the end of the year. We have a limited amount of time and probably cannot afford the time for our students to work through several complete assignments involving the double entry, trial balance, final accounts and the closing of the ledger accounts. The result is that sometimes the students have only a vague knowledge of what happens to the remaining ledger accounts at the year-end.

Another topic which we are sometimes guilty of neglecting is the posting of the analysis columns of a petty cash book to the appropriate ledger accounts. Examination scripts show that candidates are usually able to make the entries in a petty cash book to record payments. Problems often arise, however, in transferring the totals of the analysis columns into the appropriate expense accounts and transferring a payment into an individual creditor's account. Students also sometimes fail to appreciate that the amounts received by the petty cashier to restore the imprest amount actually have double entries in the main cash book.

A similar situation occurs with journal entries. Students often do not appreciate that these entries need to be recorded in the ledger. Once a journal entry has been completed, many students believe that no further entries are required for that particular transaction.

It is useful to prepare short assignments specifically on aspects such as those mentioned above which tend to be overlooked, or to ensure they are included in other assignments – see the example on page 39.

Example of short assignment involving closing off ledger accounts

The following can be written on a handout, on which the students can complete the accounts as instructed

The following are some of the accounts in the general ledger of James Langbar.

Capital account
2004
Jan 1 Balance b/d   50 000

Drawings account

2004
Dec 31 Balance b/d   13 500

Stock account

2004
Jan 1 Balance b/d   8 200

Purchases account

2004
Dec 31 Total to date   45 200

Carriage inwards account

2004
Dec 31 Total to date   2 117

Rent account

2004
Dec 31 Total to date   4 200

Rent received account
2004
Dec 31 Total to date   1 800

Close the above accounts at 31 December 2004 as appropriate. You are informed that the stock at 31 December 2004 is valued at $3700 and that the net profit for the year was $11 750.

Teaching skills in Accounting

Teacher activity 4.3

Compose a petty cash book assignment. Include the settlement of one or two small amounts due to creditors.

Ask the students to complete the petty cash book and also to make the necessary entries in the main cash book and the ledger accounts.

Teacher activity 4.4

Compose an assignment based on journal entries. This could involve opening journal entries, correction of errors, or simply transactions which would not be recorded in any other book of prime entry.

Ask the students to complete the journal entries and also to make the appropriate entries in the ledger accounts.

Another practice which is useful is to ask the students to work through an exercise that includes all the principal points of that topic. At the end of teaching the main principles of double entry I ask the students to complete an assignment which includes all the main points – cash and credit sales and purchases, sales and purchases returns, expenses and incomes, contra items, dishonoured cheques, bad debts and so on. Similarly, after teaching elementary final accounts (before year-end adjustments), I ask the students to work through an exercise containing all the main points – sales and purchases returns, carriage inwards and outwards, expenses and gains and so on.

Example of a double entry assignment which includes most of the main transactions.

For use before introducing purchases, sales and returns books.

Miriam Samba is a trader. On 1 January 2004 she had the following assets and liabilities:
   Bank $6000, Premises $52 500, Loan from finance company $4500, Capital $75 000, Fixtures and equipment $12 000, Stock $9000, Creditor – Shilongo Stores $300, Debtors – Tom Kamati $150, Amina Khan $540

The transactions for January 2004 were as follows:
Jan
3 Bought motor vehicle, $6800, and paid by cheque
5 Withdrew cash from bank, $450, for office use
6 Purchased stationery, $70, paying in cash
   Paid motor expenses in cash, $180
8 Received a cheque for $200 for rent from a tenant
10 Cash sales $590
13 Paid a cheque to Shilongo Stores for the amount due less 2% cash discount
14 Paid wages in cash, $190
16 Bought goods, $720, paying by cheque
17 Received a cheque from Tom Kamati to settle his account
20 Sold goods, $790, on credit to Metwali Traders
22 Received a cheque from Amina Khan in full settlement
25 Tom Kamati's cheque was returned by the bank marked R/D
26 Cash sales, $990, of which $750 was paid into the bank
27 Metwali Traders returned goods, $60
28 Paid wages in cash, $200
   Bought goods, $1100, on credit from Saleh Ahmed
30 Returned goods, $90, to Saleh Ahmed
31 Tom Kamati's account was written off

Record the above transactions in the ledgers and cash book of Miriam Samba. Extract a trial balance as at 31 January 2004.

The introduction of a closing stock (say $9060) means that this exercise could also be used for the preparation of final accounts and the closing of the ledger accounts.

Teacher activity 4.5

Compose a trial balance of a sole trader from which the students can be asked to prepare a set of final accounts. You should aim to include all the items the students have covered at that point in the syllabus – sales and purchases returns, goods for own use, carriage inwards and outwards, discount allowed and received, expenses and gains, bad debts written off and so on.

Encouraging understanding rather than learning by rote

Students of Accounting must be taught the basic principles and techniques which have to be applied to each topic. We are not just concerned with the final 'answer' to a calculation, but with how the information is recorded. It is not a subject where each individual can use their own methods. If this occurred, only the person who actually prepared the accounting statements would be able to understand them! We must teach our students to apply the commonly accepted accounting principles.

Obviously, not all the students will appreciate *why* they are doing things in a particular way. Even after several attempts at explaining certain principles, I have sometimes had to abandon the explanation and simply ask such students to make the necessary entries. Sometimes weeks (or even months) later, a student will come to me delighted that he/she has finally realised the significance of those entries.

Answers to theory questions on examination papers show that some students have memorised the information but are unable to apply those facts to a given situation. An example of this is the errors not revealed by a trial balance: students can often recite the six errors, but cannot actually give appropriate explanations and examples. A similar remark can be made in relation to accounting principles: students can often name them, but cannot define and apply these principles. Whilst learning by rote can play a part in examination revision, we must try to give our students every opportunity to apply the theoretical aspects of accounting. Even short assignments lasting 10–15 minutes can play a useful part – see the example below.

Example of a short practical exercise on errors not revealed by a trial balance

Students are supplied with the following assignment, together with a completed answer which contains various errors. Working alone or in pairs, they must identify the errors, stating the type of error in each case.

Alice Grey commenced business on 1 February 2004. She opened a business bank account and paid in capital of $50 000.

The transactions for the first two weeks of trading were as follows:
Feb
- 2 Purchased goods, $2000, on credit from Barry Smith
- 4 Paid rent for premises, $1000, by cheque
- 7 Cash sales, $840, paid into the bank
     Paid wages of assistants by cheque, $750
- 10 Sold goods, $650, on credit to Bettafit

12 Paid Barry Smith $2000 by cheque
13 Cash sales, $980, paid into the bank
14 Paid wages of assistants, as 7 February, by cheque

Enter the above transactions in the appropriate accounts and prepare a trial balance on 14 February 2004.

Worked assignment containing errors

Dr			Cr	Dr					Cr
	Alice Grey Capital account					Bettafit account			
	2004			2004					
	Feb 1 Bank		50 000	Feb 10 Sales	560				
	Purchases account					Bank account			
2004				2004			2004		
Feb 2 B Smith	2 000			Feb 1 Capital	50 000		Feb 4 Premises	1 000	
				12 Barry			7 Wages	750	
	Bobby Smith account			Smith	2 000		14 Wages	730	
	2004			13 Sales	960		14 Balance		
	Feb 2 Purchases	2 000					c/d	50 480	
					52 960			52 960	
	Premises account			Feb15 Balance					
2004				b/d	50 480				
Feb 4 Bank	1 000								
	Wages account				Trial Balance as at 14 February 2004				
2004									
Feb 7 Bank	750						Dr		Cr
14 Bank	750			Capital					50 000
	1 500			Purchases			2 000		
	Sales account			Bobby Smith					2 000
	2004			Premises			1 000		
	Feb 10 Bettafit		560	Wages			1 500		
	13 Bank		980	Sales					1 540
			1 540	Barry Smith					2 000
	Barry Smith account			Bettafit			560		
	2004			Bank			50 480		
	Feb 12 Bank	2 000					55 540		55 540

Please refer to the end of the chapter for a list of the errors.

Teaching skills in Accounting 43

> **Teacher activity 4.6**
>
> Prepare a short assignment on the application of accounting principles (concepts and conventions).
>
> Give a list of situations and ask the students to identify the principle being applied in each case. Multiple-choice questions often provide useful scenarios on which this assignment can be based.

> **Teacher activity 4.7**
>
> Prepare a short assignment on the application of the different methods of depreciation.
>
> Give details of three or four fixed assets and ask the students to state which method of depreciation is most appropriate in each case, and justify that statement.

Those new to teaching often worry about making an error when demonstrating something on the board. Even very experienced teachers can make errors sometimes. Use any errors as teaching points. If a student points out the error, praise him/her for spotting it. If no-one spots the error, ask the students if anyone can spot the 'deliberate error'. Students often take great delight in spotting mistakes made by the teacher! If no-one has spotted an error in a double entry exercise, I sometimes do not draw their attention to it immediately, but wait until the Trial Balance fails to balance and then ask them to look for the error. A similar procedure can be followed when you spot an error in the Trading and Profit and Loss Account – you can wait until the Balance Sheet fails to balance before asking the students to find the error.

Encouraging interpretation of accounting statements

Whilst students need to be taught the principles of preparing accounting statements, it is also important to encourage understanding of those statements. The topic of interpretation of final accounts will usually have to be taught quite late in the course when the students are in a better position to appreciate the principles involved. There is no reason, however, why elementary interpretation cannot be introduced at every suitable opportunity during the course. Students are often able to work things out for themselves if we ask the right questions or provide suitable prompting – see the elementary interpretation of final accounts on page 45.

Example of introducing elementary interpretation of final accounts

For use after teaching the basic principles of final accounts (before year-end adjustments)

M. Ali is a trader. He does not have any accounting knowledge, but attempted to prepare a trial balance at the end of his financial year on 31 March 2004.

M. Ali
Trial Balance for the year ended 31 March 2004

	Dr $	Cr $
Capital		7 500
Bank overdraft	3 500	
Cash	200	
Debtors		4 300
Creditors	5 750	
Purchases	11 000	
Sales		16 700
Purchases returns	820	
Sales returns		1 180
Furniture and equipment	2 400	
Wages	6 900	
Rent	1 600	
Drawings		4 000
Sundry expenses	1 430	
Discount received	220	
Discount allowed		140
	33 820	33 820

Stock 1 April 2003 amounted to $1340
Stock 31 March 2004 amounted to $2500

Prepare a corrected trial balance.

Prepare a Trading and Profit and Loss Account for the year ended 31 March 2004 and a Balance Sheet as at 31 March 2004.

Providing a trial balance containing errors is useful for a quick revision of which items are debits and which are credits.

The Profit and Loss Account will show a net loss. The Balance Sheet will show a shortage of working capital.

Introduce interpretation of final accounts by asking questions such as:
- What is the significance of the net loss for the business and for the trader?
- Why do you think the trader made a net loss?
- How could the net loss have been prevented, or reduced?
- What does it mean when current liabilities exceed current assets?
- What is the significance of this shortage of working capital for the business?
- Why has this shortage arisen?
- How can the trader remedy the situation?

> **Teacher activity 4.8**
>
> Compose an assignment involving the preparation of a two- or three-column cash book for one month – with or without postings to the ledger accounts.
>
> Ensure that there is a bank overdraft at the end of the month. This could be caused by a combination of a significant purchase of fixed assets, large drawings and a dishonoured cheque.
>
> As a question and answer exercise after the completion of the assignment, ask questions relating to this overdraft, such as:
> - What is the significance of a credit balance on the bank account?
> - What are the consequences of this bank overdraft?
> - How could this situation have been avoided?
> - How can the situation be remedied in the short term?
> - What steps can be taken to ensure that it does not occur again?

Learning activities

In addition to teacher-led learning, students appreciate the opportunity to think for themselves and to be able to apply the principles they have been taught. Such activities allow the teacher the chance to talk to individual students, knowing that the others are profitably occupied. These activities are also a good opportunity to see whether students are applying the principles they have been taught and where further emphasis is required. I always try to vary the activities so that students sometimes work alone and sometimes in groups. If possible, try to bring an element of realism into the activities, so that students appreciate the practical aspects of the theory.

Example activity

For use after the teaching of business documents and books of original entry.

This activity takes a lot of preparation – but once completed can be used for several years with different classes of students.

Working in groups of 2 or 3, the students will be asked to write up the books of original entry from 'actual' business documents and make the necessary ledger entries. You can download pro-forma documents from websites such as www.osbornebooks.co.uk, prepare them yourself, or maybe the students could produce them in their keyboard lessons. This could also be combined with a previous assignment (based on questions set on IGCSE Paper 2) where the students fill in missing information on invoices, credit notes etc.

For a sole trader for one month:
- assume that there are 4 or 5 debtors and the same number of creditors;
- prepare 7 or 8 sales invoices, some including trade discount;
- prepare 7 or 8 purchases invoices, some including trade discount;
- prepare 3 credit notes sent to customers, some including trade discount;
- prepare 3 credit notes received from suppliers, some including trade discount;
- prepare 3 or 4 cheque book counterfoils for payments to suppliers, some including cash discount;
- prepare 3 or 4 paying-in book counterfoils for receipts from customers, some including cash discount;
- prepare a cheque made payable to the trader, returned from the bank with 'R/D' written across the face.

It is not necessary to collate these documents – let the students do that.

The students have to make the necessary entries in the books of prime entry and make the appropriate postings to the ledger accounts.

The debtor and creditor accounts could also have existing balances brought down from the previous month. If the division of the ledger has been taught, students would be expected to show the ledger accounts in the appropriate ledgers.

> **Teacher activity 4.9**
>
> Devise a learning activity for the preparation of a two- or three-column cash book using cheque counterfoils and paying-in slip counterfoils. Totals from the cash till could also be included for the cash sales. A dishonoured cheque could also be included.
>
> Aim to have about 10 receipts and 10 payments.

> **Teacher activity 4.10**
>
> Devise a learning activity for the preparation of a petty cash book using petty cash vouchers. This could also involve transferring the totals of the analysis columns to the ledger.

Preparing an adequate amount of material

Students do not all work at the same pace. We must plan our lessons around what we consider to be the average students. When considering how much material will be required it is useful to consider the following criteria:
- What *must* be achieved in the lesson.
- What *should* be achieved in the lesson.
- What *could* be achieved in the lesson.

Those students who work at a slower pace will sometimes have to complete an assignment in their own time. The more able students will need to be provided with additional assignments. It is important that quicker students are not expected to simply wait for the others to catch up. I usually have a few short assignments of medium/hard level of difficulty available for these more able students. 'Do you never run out of things for us to do?' students often ask.

One device which I use to keep the class working at approximately the same pace is to ask them to complete small sections of an assignment, rather than asking them to complete it all in one go. On a double entry assignment we may all work through the first few entries together, and then I will ask the students to complete the next three or four double entries on their own (making sure that these do not involve any unfamiliar items). I may then ask individual students what entries they have made and write these on the board. Sometimes I ask the students to make the entries in the accounts on the board – but this can result in the board becoming a little 'messy'! The students then make any corrections necessary before we go on to the next item. I follow a similar pattern with final accounts, asking students to list the expenses in the Profit and Loss

Account, list the fixed assets, and so on, and checking at the end of each section that all the students have made the correct entries.

It is very easy to overestimate the amount of material you will get through in a lesson, but this is preferable to not having enough material. There is nothing worse than seeing the students completing the last planned assignment with the clock still showing that there are another 15 minutes left before the end of the lesson! Experience helps us to judge how long it will take to deliver a lesson on a certain topic. Detailed lesson notes often prove invaluable in future years as they show how long was spent on certain topics.

I am sure that we have all experienced the situation when students deliberately set out to distract the teacher from the aim of the lesson by asking completely unrelated questions. Where these are quite obviously completely unrelated to the subject of Accounting, I refer the students to the library or the Internet. Where they are based on Accounting I find it better to briefly answer the question. If the question involves a topic which is on the syllabus but which will arise in a later lesson, I briefly outline the topic and explain that this will be covered in more detail later. If the question involves a topic which is outside the syllabus and which will not arise in a later lesson, I give a much shorter explanation of the topic and explain that this is covered on a more advanced course.

I am sure that all teachers worry about being asked a question which they are unable to answer. In such a situation I find it best to admit that I cannot answer the question. If you try to talk your way out of the problem, students will soon realise that you are unsure of the answer! Far better to explain that it is a long time since you studied, or taught, that particular topic. If you promise to look up the problem and give them an answer in the next lesson, do make sure that you keep that promise.

LOOKING BACK

In this chapter we have discussed lesson planning and learning activities.

Reflect on your lessons.
- Can they be improved, and, if so, how?
- Do you try to vary the format of the lessons?
- Do you try to ensure that your students appreciate the interrelationship of the separate topics within the syllabus?
- Are you doing enough to encourage your students to understand and interpret the accounting statements they are preparing?

Errors in the worked assignment on page 43
Feb
2	Bobby Smith account credited instead of Barry Smith account	Error of commission
4	Premises account debited instead of rent account	Error of principle
7	No entries appear in the books for this transaction	Error of omission
10	$560 entered in both accounts instead of $650	Error of original entry
12	Barry Smith account credited instead of debited and bank account debited instead of credited	Error of complete reversal
13	Bank account debited with $960 instead of $980	Compensating error
14	Bank account credited with $730 instead of $750	

5 Assessing skills in Accounting

This chapter concentrates on the ways in which we can assess skills in accounting. We will consider the two types of assessment:
- **formative assessment** – assessment *for* learning;
- **summative assessment** – assessment *of* learning.

Formative assessment
This consists of any means of assessing the skills the students have acquired, and can take place at any time during the course. Giving assignments for the students to complete in class or at home, or a more formal 'class test' are ways in which progress can be assessed.

If you choose to give a 'test' to be completed in class, you must decide whether or not to give the students warning that this is to take place. In either case, it is wise to explain to the students the reasons for such a test.

In the first week of the course, I always explain to my classes that they will be getting lots of pieces of work to complete at home and also some to be completed in class. I am a great believer in 'practice makes perfect': the more work a student completes during the course, the greater chance he/she has of passing the examination at the end of the course. Students cannot expect to pass an Accounting examination by simply revising on the day before the examination.

Planning the assessment
The assessments need to be carefully thought out so that there are sections which test students of all abilities. Ideally questions should be graded, starting with a simple one and progressing to more difficult ones.

It is preferable to set questions which are independent of each other. Constant carrying forward of the students' own figures means that marking is much more time-consuming. More importantly, a student who fails to complete the first question may be unable to attempt the subsequent questions.

The assessments do not, of course, all need to follow the same format. Try to give as much variety as possible.

Marking the assessment

The way the assessments are marked may be determined to some extent by the amount of time available. Where you have a full timetable and large classes, you will probably not have the time to mark every assessment your students complete.

Try to vary ways of marking the assessments. A short 20–30 minute assessment in class can be structured so that students can mark their own work or exchange books and mark the work of another student.

A longer, structured question is probably more suitable for homework or a class assessment which is to be handed in for marking. Where the students are working through an assessment in class, you can check each student's work as you are walking round the classroom. This has the advantage of allowing you to discuss points individually with the students.

I do think that it is important that you mark as many assessments as you can. This is especially important where the assessment consists of structured questions, for example a set of final accounts or a set of ledger accounts recording depreciation and disposal of fixed assets. We cannot expect students to be able to apply the marking scheme accurately to such questions. These questions often involve the application of accounting principles to a given situation where the 'own figure rule' needs to be applied. As teachers we are only too well aware that an error in a set of accounts or in an accounting statement may affect later figures. For example, when a set of final accounts is being prepared an incorrect sales figure will affect the gross profit in the Trading Account and the net profit in both the Profit and Loss Account and the Balance Sheet. A student would be penalised for the incorrect sales figure, but the own figure rule would apply to the gross profit and the net profit, as they are incorrect solely because of an earlier error.

Marking the assessments also gives you the opportunity to see how individual students are progressing: it is easy to overlook one individual's progress when an assessment is marked by the students themselves, and there is the possibility of students 'cheating' when they mark their own work!

Teacher activity 5.1

Draw up a grid for the school year showing the teaching weeks, holiday periods and examination dates.

Write in the dates when each of your classes will be set an assessment (to complete either in class or at home) which you will mark.

This will ensure that your work is distributed evenly and you do not have all the classes submitting assessments for marking at the same time.

(In situations where students are provided with an assessment timetable for all subjects, your plan need only distinguish between those assessments for marking by the teacher and those for marking by the students.)

Feedback from assessments

Whatever form the assessment takes, it should provide valuable feedback for both the students and the teacher.

It is essential that you provide some feedback for your students. This will show each student which topics, or aspects of a topic, they need to spend more time on in order to improve their skills. Where the assessment is marked in class, you will be able to provide explanations as you go through the answers. Where you have marked the assessment, it is important that you put corrections and comments on each individual piece of work. Students can then see not only *where* they have gone wrong, but also *how* the answer should have been prepared.

The results of the assessment should also be used as feedback by the teacher. These results can provide useful information about which topics need to be revised by individual students and which topics could be more profitably revised with the whole class.

Teacher activity 5.2

Evaluate an assessment your students have completed. Consider the following points:
- Did the assessment indicate that you need to revise some or all of the work with the whole class?
- Did the assessment indicate that certain students need help to overcome problems in certain areas?
- Were there any unexpected outcomes in the form of unexpected answers, or unexpected student performance?
- Is the assessment suitable for use in the future in its present format, or could it be improved?

Setting assessments

You can always make use of questions on past examination papers for setting assessments.

The first questions at the end of each chapter in the endorsed textbook for IGCSE Accounting are short-answer questions which are suitable for use in assessments which are to be marked by the students themselves. Similarly, questions on IGCSE Paper 2, which involve short written answers or completion of accounting statements by filling in 'boxes', are also ideal for this purpose.

In Appendix C on pages 75–80 you will find examples of two short assessment tests containing graded questions which are suitable for students to mark themselves.

> **Teacher activity 5.3**
>
> Construct a short assessment for use after teaching books of original entry and business documents.
>
> The assessment should take students about 30 minutes to complete, and should be suitable for self-marking by the students.
>
> Try to ensure that each section of the assessment is independent and does not rely too much on figures from other sections.

When using a question from a textbook do check that the answer is not in the back of the book! If you only have a limited amount of past examination papers, it may be sensible to reserve these for 'mock' examinations and revision at the end of the course.

Wherever possible try to include more than one assessment objective (skill) in each question or assessment. For example, the preparation of a cash book (Skill A) can be combined with a short theory question on why a bank overdraft has arisen or how it could have been avoided (Skill C). Similarly, a partnership Appropriation Account (Skill B) can be combined with a short theory question about the contents of a partnership agreement or the advantages of admitting a new partner (Skill A).

In Appendix C (pages 80–2) you will find examples of two structured assessment questions which are suitable for marking by the teacher.

Summative assessment

This assessment of learning usually takes place at the end of a module of work, the end of a school term, or the end of the school year. The final examination will obviously be the externally set IGCSE or O level examination, but the students may also sit internally assessed school examinations before then.

Setting external examination papers

Examination papers are usually set by the principal examiner, or a highly experienced senior examiner. Each paper must reflect:

- good syllabus coverage;
- no overlaps with the other papers which form part of the examination;
- a balance of skills to conform to those required by the specification grid;
- an appropriate balance of the core and extended syllabus (where applicable);
- a suitable degree of difficulty.

The draft paper passes through various checking and evaluation processes before it is finally printed.

Setting internal examination papers

I always base internal examinations on the actual external examination my students are to sit. It may even be possible to use a past examination paper in its entirety under simulated examination conditions. In many cases, however, you will not have completed the syllabus when the internal examination is taken, so papers will have to be adapted. Even if you decide to compose the whole of the internal examination paper yourself, try to model it on the actual external paper. This helps your students familiarise themselves with the format and style of questions on the examination paper. Your students will have become used to the way you phrase questions and what you expect, but they need a wider experience of how questions may be formulated.

When setting an examination paper, try to make sure that it covers as much of the syllabus as possible and has the right balance between the skills we discussed earlier.

Ideally the questions should be set to reflect the range of ability of the whole class – not just the more able students. Where there are several teachers teaching the same course, why not work together and prepare one examination paper for all the classes? This can work very well as the other teachers are often able to spot pitfalls (which you cannot always see in your own work) and suggest improvements and alternative answers which may be acceptable.

Marking of external examination papers

Examination papers are marked by a team of assistant examiners under the guidance of the principal examiner for each paper.

After the examination, the principal examiner and the team leaders study as many scripts as possible before a coordination meeting which is attended by all the examiners. At this meeting all the possible variations of answers will be discussed and agreement reached on how the mark scheme (which was drawn up when the paper was set) will be applied to such answers. A final version of the mark scheme is agreed at the meeting and all examiners mark a selection of photocopied scripts using this final mark scheme.

Checks are constantly carried out by the principal examiner and the team leaders during the marking process to ensure that all the assistant examiners are marking consistently and uniformly. Where an assistant examiner is in doubt about the validity of an answer, advice must be sought from the principal examiner or the team leader. An examiner cannot take a decision independently as this could affect the overall uniformity of marking.

After the grade boundaries have been fixed, scripts of those candidates who are possibly at risk of being awarded an incorrect grade are re-marked by a senior examiner.

> **Teacher activity 5.4**
>
> Familiarise yourself with the abbreviations which commonly appear on published mark schemes.
>
> Are you familiar with the following abbreviations which are used by examiners?
>
> - C/F (sometimes shown as 'C/F only')
> - O/F
> - O/F if no extraneous items (sometimes shown as 'O/F if no aliens')
> - D
> - R
>
> *The answers are in Appendix E.*

Marking internal examination papers

When selecting – or composing – a structured question, decide how you are going to award the marks before you actually start marking the students' work. You may be surprised at how many different versions of the same answer there are – some of which you have never thought of! Whilst allowing for correct answers arrived at by acceptable methods, which were not actually anticipated, try to stick to the mark scheme. This will mean that you will not be influenced by the student's name at the top of the page, and will be more consistent in your marking. Consistency can also be maintained by marking Question 1 for all the examinees, then marking Question 2 and so on. Remember to mark what is presented to you – not what you think the student meant to write.

If you decide to use a past examination paper, obtain a copy of the mark scheme for it. The mark schemes are published and are also available online. (See Appendix B for addresses). Why not think about how *you* would allocate the marks before you consult the official mark scheme?

Teacher activity 5.5

Prepare an answer and a mark scheme for the structured assessment question below. You should aim to have a total of 20 marks.

Compare your answer and mark scheme with the one in Appendix E.

Structured assessment question – based on a question on IGCSE Paper 2 June 2000

a) Name **one** accounting principle which is being observed when a provision for doubtful debts is maintained.
b) Explain the difference between *bad debts* and a *provision for doubtful debts*.
c) State **two** ways in which a business may decide the amount of its provision for doubtful debts.
d) The following relates to the business of Mary Maranga, who writes her accounts up to 31 March each year.

	$
Trade debtors 1 April 2003	40 000
Trade debtors 31 March 2004	46 000
Bad debts written off in the year ended 31 March 2004	800

The provision for doubtful debts is maintained at $2\frac{1}{2}\%$ of the trade debtors at the end of each year.

(i) Write up the bad debts account and the provision for doubtful debts account in Mary Maranga's ledger for the year ended 31 March 2004, showing clearly the amounts transferred to the Profit and Loss Account.

(Where a traditional 'T' account is used it should be balanced and the balance brought down on 1 April 2004. Where a three-column running balance account is used the balance column should be updated after each transaction.)

(ii) Show the relevant extract from Mary Maranga's Balance Sheet as at 31 March 2004. Clearly indicate the section of the Balance Sheet where the entry will appear.

e) Suggest **three** ways in which Mary Maranga may reduce the possibility of bad debts.

If the examination is to be taken by several classes, the marking will be shared by all the class teachers. Why not arrange for one teacher to mark Question 1 for all the candidates, another teacher Question 2 and so on? This should ensure that the marking scheme is applied consistently. My colleagues and I operated such a policy very successfully when I worked in a large college where six groups all followed the same syllabus and all sat a common term-end examination.

Multiple-choice questions

We must not forget that multiple-choice questions can be used for both formative and summative assessments. Many accounting examinations contain a compulsory paper consisting of multiple-choice items. Such a question paper allows wide syllabus coverage and facilitates specific syllabus topics and assessment objectives to be targeted.

These question papers are marked electronically. The answer to each of the questions is checked by several people before being keyed into the system.

Teacher activity 5.6

Familiarise yourself with the terminology often used in multiple-choice items.

Are you familiar with the following terms?
- stem
- options
- key
- distractors

The answers are in Appendix E.

I believe in introducing students to multiple-choice questions early in the course, so that they are quite familiar with them by the time they are due to sit the external examination. Initially I work through a few verbally with the class, and then gradually introduce a few into written assessments. Towards the end of the course I may give the class a set of 20 or so questions to be completed within a set time (based on the time allowed for the external examination paper).

If you only have a limited number of past examination papers, it may be necessary to compose some multiple-choice items yourself. Study those in the published papers so that you are familiar with the style of question. The basic principles of setting multiple-choice questions are as follows:

The stem

Do
- be brief
- ask a direct question
- use clear language

Avoid
- negative answers if possible
- sentence completion
- asking for the student's opinion

The options

Do
- check that they are on the syllabus
- arrange in a logical order:
    alphabetically
    numerically
    pairs of options
    tabular form

Avoid
- overlapping of options
- giving a clue in the key
- having one longer than the others

The distractors

Do
- ensure that they are plausible
- ensure that numerical distractors are derived from possible miscalculations

The key

Do
- ensure that this is the only possible correct answer

Teacher activity 5.7

Consider the following multiple-choice items. Why are they unsuitable for inclusion in a multiple-choice assessment?

1. In which order should current assets be arranged in a Balance Sheet?
    a) Bank, stock, debtors, cash
    b) Cash, bank, debtors, stock
    c) Debtors, bank, stock, cash
    d) Stock, debtors, bank, cash

2. Businesses X and Y both have a gross profit percentage of 20%.

	X	Y
	$	$
Sales	90 000	30 000
General expenses	9 000	3 600

Which statement is correct?
a) X is more efficient than Y.
b) X has a lower net profit percentage than Y.
c) Y has a higher net profit percentage than X.
d) Y is more efficient than X.

3. A trial balance fails to agree because the debit side exceeded the credit side by $5000. A suspense account is opened into which the difference is entered. Which error does not involve double entry in order to correct it?
   a) Goods bought by cheque, $400, credited in the cash book but not entered in the purchases account
   b) Rent paid, $100, entered on the credit side of the cash book, but also credited to the rent account in error
   c) The debit side of the cash book being overcast by $2000
   d) The sales account, containing a balance of $4000, but which was entered in the trial balance as $400

The answers are in Appendix E.

LOOKING BACK

In this chapter we have discussed the ways in which skills in accounting can be assessed.

Reflect on the classes you teach.
- What is the balance between formative and summative assessment in each course?
- Which methods of assessment do you use regularly?
- Do you give your students the opportunity to practise on past examination papers (including multiple-choice)?
- Can you improve the structure of the assessments and the mark schemes for those assessments?
- Are you providing adequate feedback to your students?
- Are you making the most appropriate use of the results of the assessments to improve your teaching and assessment methods?

6 Preparing students for Accounting examinations

It is part of our job as teachers to do our best to ensure that our students are adequately prepared for the external examination.

Key words used in Accounting examinations

If you study external examination papers in Accounting, you will find various key words (or command words) are used in the questions. These words direct the candidates on how to answer the question. They cover such words as 'draw up', 'explain', 'prepare' and so on. Appendix D gives a list of some key words and phrases used in Accounting examinations.

Students need to be able to recognise these words and understand what the question requires.

Published syllabus support materials

'Am I teaching to the right level?' is a common worry for teachers. If you are an experienced teacher, or have been preparing groups of students for the same examination for several years, you will be familiar with the standards required.

> **Teacher activity 6.1 for experienced teachers**
>
> Think of the most able student in last year's class. What grade did you expect that student to achieve in the final examination? What grade did that student actually achieve?
>
> Repeat this process in relation to the least able student and an average student in last year's class.
>
> Compare the students in your present class with those in the parallel class last year. Use this as a guide to forecasting what the present students will achieve in the final examination.

If you are a new teacher, or new to a particular syllabus, you will naturally be concerned about teaching to an appropriate level. CIE publish material to support the syllabus which may be of assistance to teachers in this respect.

Standards Booklet

To support each syllabus CIE produces a Standards Booklet. The aim of these booklets is to show how different levels of candidates' performance relate to the subject's assessment skills. They contain examination questions and a number of extracts from candidates' examination scripts, chosen to illustrate a range of performances. These are not intended to be 'model' answers but are examples of the ways in which the answers earned marks. Appropriate extracts from the examiners' report for that particular examination are included, together with comments by the principal examiner on each script extract.

The combination of questions, students' answers and comments by the principal examiner should ensure that these booklets are basically a guide to the process of assessment applied in the external examination for the particular syllabus.

Examiners' report

We have already mentioned the fact that CIE, in common with most other examination boards, publish a report on each examination paper.

In addition to general comments about each component paper of the examination, the report contains comments on specific questions. Obtain a copy of the report and read it in conjunction with the actual question papers and marking schemes. This should be regarded not only as an account of that particular examination, but also as a guide for students sitting examinations in the future. The report will indicate where many candidates lost marks and which topics require greater emphasis.

Let us take the report on the IGCSE Accounting papers for June 2003 as an example.

The comments on Paper 1 (Multiple-choice questions) indicate that, statistically, none of the items was too easy, but ten items proved to be too difficult. An individual comment is given about each of these ten items. The report on Paper 2 indicates that candidates performed well overall. However, some candidates appeared to be unfamiliar with basic techniques such as writing up a three-column cash book and posting the totals of the discount columns to the general ledger.

The underlying theme of the report on Paper 3 is that, whilst there were many good candidates, others lost marks through carelessness and lack of attention to detail. Reference is also made to questions which have been asked on previous occasions (such as the disadvantages of having insufficient working capital and reducing the risk of bad debts) but which are still being answered incorrectly.

Reading such reports makes us aware of candidates' overall performance in the external examination and gives us an insight into areas where improvements may be made. We must try to relate this to our students and incorporate it into our teaching practices wherever possible.

> **Teacher activity 6.2**
>
> Work through a past examination paper for the course your students are following.
>
> Make brief notes on the areas where you consider your students would have problems, any alternative answers which you consider could be acceptable and so on.
>
> Obtain a copy of the examiners' report for the paper and compare what the principal examiner says about each question with your own comments.

Revision strategies

Where students have been given regular assessments in the form of assignments for completion either at home or in class, they will be accustomed to examination questions. Allowing students access to past papers will enable them to become familiar with the style and format of complete examination papers. Students should be encouraged to work through a number of such papers before sitting the external examination.

It is still wise, however, to allow some time at the end of the course which can be devoted to revision. Even the more able students often need reminding of some of the topics covered early in the course!

Each teacher will have their own methods of organising the revision work with their classes. Whatever method you adopt, do try to go over all the topics of the syllabus – however briefly.

I ask the students to suggest topics which they would like to revise. A system of tutorials can then be organised with students joining in as their chosen topic is revised. The rest of the classroom is in the form of a workshop where students are free to revise other topics.

In addition to asking students to suggest topics, I prepare a list of all the topics covered during the year(s). Alongside each topic I suggest at least two questions from past examination papers which the students can work through at their own pace. A few entries from such a revision list are given on page 64.

Revision List			
Form 5B			November 2003
Topic	Suggested Revision Questions		
	Question 1	Question 2	Question 3
Journal entries	IGCSE June 2002 Paper 2 No 4	IGCSE Nov 2002 Paper 3 No 1	
Partnership accounts	IGCSE Nov 2002 Paper 2 No 5	IGCSE Nov 2002 Paper 3 No 4	
Ratios	IGCSE June 2002 Paper 2 No 5	IGCSE Nov 2002 Paper 3 No 5	

A lot of preparation is involved in completing and duplicating the list and ensuring that all the students have copies of the appropriate examination questions. However, I have always found it time well spent, and the basis of the list can be used in future years.

I usually make the answers available in class for the students to consult. Whilst the students are working through the list of suggested questions, I spend most of the time walking round the classroom discussing points with individual students. The students are not the only ones who are working hard just before the external examination!

Teacher activity 6.3

Prepare a revision list for your class to work through before they sit the external examination.

Aim to include at least two questions from past examination papers on each main topic.

Try to ensure that the selected questions test different aspects of each topic.

Examination hints for students

I think it is important that our students feel reasonably confident when they enter the examination room. Many of them will obviously be anxious and rather nervous. I am sure that, like me, you talk about the examination with your students and try to impress on them the basic examination techniques. The fifteen points that I try to emphasise to my students are shown on page 65. Some of these are obvious to us, as teachers, but not necessarily as obvious to the students.

Rather than waiting until just before the external examination, I try to draw the students' attention to these basic points at suitable opportunities during the year. For example, the opportunity often arises to explain that a student could probably have gained some of the available marks in a class assessment if only some calculations had been shown. Similarly, students are often tempted to do more than is required, e.g. showing the double entries into the ledger when only a cash book is required, or listing four advantages of admitting a new partner when only two are required, and so on. These serve as examples of losing valuable time doing something that is not required. If I have an accounting statement on the board, a set of final accounts for example, I may illustrate to the students how the majority of the available marks can still be earned even though an item, say an adjustment for doubtful debts, is omitted.

Hints for Accounting examination candidates

- Be sure that you enter for the correct options.
- Be well prepared – cover the whole of the syllabus thoroughly; work through as many examples and past papers as possible.
- On the day of the exam allow plenty of time to get to the venue.
- Read the question paper through carefully, and then read each question again before attempting to answer it.
- Allocate the time according to the marks per question.
- Start with the question which you feel most confident about.
- Do not over-run on time per question.
- Answer the question being asked.
- Do not do more than is required: you may not lose marks but you will lose time.
- Attempt all the questions that are required.
- It is better to attempt all the required questions and only part-complete them than to do one or two questions perfectly.
- If there is an item within a question that you are not familiar with, do not abandon the question. Omit the particular item.
- If you wish to re-attempt an answer, do not cross out the original answer until you have completed the new version.
- Do show calculations where appropriate – you may gain some marks even if the final answer is incorrect.
- Finally, if you finish the examination early, do not leave the exam room until you have checked all your work thoroughly.

Where marks are lost in Accounting examinations

It may be appropriate at this point to consider where candidates lose marks in examinations – apart from the errors in the actual accounting principles and practice. If we, as teachers, are aware of how candidates lose these marks, we may be able to help our students to avoid these common pitfalls. The following are some of the most common ways in which candidates lose marks in Accounting examinations.

Failing to show calculations

Even where calculations are not specifically asked for candidates are advised to show their workings. Where the final answer is incorrect, say for the calculation of a ratio, some marks may be earned for that part of the workings which is correct.

Careless errors

Many marks are wasted by candidates making careless errors. Some of these can, of course, simply be caused by the pressure arising from working under examination conditions. Such errors include the transposition of figures (for example, $4540 written as $4450) and the use of inappropriate symbols (for example $40 instead of 40%). It is not unknown for a candidate to indicate that a figure is to be deducted and then actually add that figure, or vice versa (for example writing 'sales less returns' but actually adding the returns). The omission of words such as 'net profit' and 'balance' may also cause marks to be lost.

Lack of attention to details

The omission of dates in ledger accounts and books of prime entry is an example of lack of attention to details. Similarly, using 'B' or 'BBD' for 'Balance' is not usually regarded as acceptable. When candidates are writing ratios they sometimes give an incomplete answer (for example putting '35' for the collection period for debtors instead of '35 days'). In relation to final accounts, it is disappointing to see how many candidates fail to display a Balance Sheet correctly with the assets and liabilities subdivided with suitable section headings and subtotals.

Leaving the examiner to select the correct answer

This is commonly referred to as 'hedging'. In theory questions where two items are required some candidates may give a long list of items (some correct and some incorrect) and expect the examiner to select the correct ones. Similarly, when writing up accounts, candidates who are unsure of the correct wording may leave it to the examiner to choose the correct word (for example in a ledger account the words

'Balance/Goods/Sales/Purchases' may all appear instead of just one word against the entry). Candidates also operate the policy of 'hedging' within accounts by putting an entry on both sides of a ledger account, or putting an item in both the Profit and Loss Account and the Appropriation Account. In all these cases, the candidate will lose the marks for that particular item.

Repetition

In theory questions, candidates may be asked to list a number of points. It is quite common for them to make the same point twice. For example, in an answer on how to reduce the risk of bad debts, saying 'sell more goods on a cash basis' and 'reduce credit sales' will count as one point, not two.

Not answering the question being asked

Candidates may make a factually correct statement in response to a theory question, but will not earn any marks if that statement is not the answer to the question being asked. Marks will also not be awarded if candidates simply state the obvious (for example the statement 'The Receipts and Payments Accounts show receipts and payments' will gain no marks).

> **LOOKING BACK**
>
> In this chapter we have discussed the importance of preparing students for Accounting examinations.
>
> Reflect on the following:
> - Are your students familiar with key words used in examinations?
> - Did you familiarise yourself with the published support material?
> - Did you provide your students with a suitable revision programme?
> - Did you provide your students with hints on examination techniques?
> - Did your students complete a 'mock' examination?
> - Are your students familiar with the ways in which marks can be lost in examinations?

Books for teachers

The following are suggested resources for teachers to support the delivery of the IGCSE syllabus and the O level syllabus:

Business Accounting Vol. 1, Wood, Frank & Sangster, Alan (2002) Prentice Hall, New Jersey

Business Accounting Vol. 2, Wood, Frank & Sangster, Alan (2002) Prentice Hall, New Jersey

Business Accounting, Giles, R. (2001), Nelson Thornes, Cheltenham

The Complete A–Z Accounting Handbook, Harrison, I. (2003), Hodder & Stoughton, London

Appendix B: Useful addresses

University of Cambridge International Examinations
1 Hills Road, Cambridge, CB1 2EU, United Kingdom
Telephone: +44 (0)1223 553554
Fax: +44 (0)1223 553558
Email: international@ucles.co.uk

Useful websites
CIE sites
- www.cie.org.uk
  The main CIE website

The following websites are available only to CIE centres:
- http://teachers.cie.org.uk
  The teachers' support site, which provides past papers, mark schemes and examiners' reports for IGCSE Accounting. Other items such as schemes of work will be provided in the future. To access this site you must first visit the main CIE site or email ts@ucles.org.uk.

- http://lists.ucles.org.uk/lists/listinfo/cie-accounting
  This is an email-based on-line discussion group for teachers of Accounting. To access this site you must first visit the main CIE site or email international @ucles.org.uk for joining instructions.

Other sites
Assessment material etc.
- www.bbc.co.uk/schools/gcsebitesize/business
- www.bized.ac.ukstafsup/option
- www.ool.co.uk
- www.osbornebooks.co.uk
- wps.prenhall.com/ema_uk_he_wood_busacct_9
  The companion site to *Business Accounting 1 and 2* by Frank Wood and Alan Sangster
- www.tutor2U.net

Check the material very carefully before downloading and distributing to your classes.

Make sure that it is suitable for testing the topics you wish to set as assessments for your students and does not contain material which has not yet been covered in the scheme of work.

Check the terminology used to make sure that it is precise and correct. Some sites incorrectly refer to debiting and crediting a Balance Sheet, to profit being in the form of money etc.

Publishers
- www.uk.cambridge.org/education — Cambridge University Press
- www.oup.co.uk — Oxford University Press
- www.pearsoned.co.uk — Pearson Education Books

Newspapers and magazines
- www.accountancyage.com — Accountancy Age
- www.accountingtechnician.co.uk — Accounting Technician
- www.ft.com — The Financial Times
- www.timesonline.co.uk — The Times

Professional Accounting Bodies
- www.aat.co.uk — AAT (Association of Accounting Technicians)
- www.accaglobal.com — ACCA (Association of Chartered Certified Accountants)
- www.cimaglobal.com — CIMA (Chartered Institute of Management Accountants)
- www.cipfa.org.uk — CIPFA (The Chartered Institute of Public Finance and Accountancy)
- www.icaew.co.uk — ICAEW (Institute of Chartered Accountants in England and Wales)
- www.icas.org.uk — ICAS (Institute of Chartered Accountants of Scotland)

Other accounting websites
- www.accountingweb.co.uk — accounting articles
- www.asb.org.uk — Accounting Standards Board
- www.companyreporting.com — published accounts
- www.iasb.org.uk — International Accounting Standards Board

Appendix C: Examples of assessments

A Example of a simple 'cross-subject' assessment
This assessment incorporates Accounting, Business Studies, English, and research in library or on the Internet

Students work in groups of 3 or 4.

Time allowed: $2\frac{1}{2}$–3 hours

Background information
Tariq Ali has built up a profitable electronics business. His headquarters are in .... (insert name of a town or city). Ahmed, Tariq's son, has recently completed a course in electronics and has been brought into the business. Tariq now hopes to be able to expand his business by purchasing and equipping a workshop in another town or city and putting his son in charge of the new enterprise.

All the office procedures would still be carried out at the headquarters and the wages would be calculated there and forwarded to the new branch by bank transfer.

Not having a wide business background, Tariq comes to you for some help.

Task 1
Tariq informs you that he is considering setting up his new branch in .... (insert name of town or city). He is interested in finding out more about this town (city) and asks you to find out:
a) How long does it take to get there by train from Tariq's headquarters? Is it necessary to change trains?
b) What is the estimated population?
c) What are the main products of the town (city) at the present time?
d) How many electronics factories are based there already?
e) What is the local weekly paper and on what day is it published?
f) What is the address of the nearest local television or radio station?

You should present the information in a precise and informative manner.

Task 2
Tariq is wondering how to finance his new venture, which will probably cost in the region of $50 000. He asks you to make a list of the institutions you think would be prepared to lend this amount of money.

You decide to add a separate list of other ways in which Tariq could raise the money without obtaining a loan.

Task 3
Assume that Tariq decided to ask his bank (give name and address of a bank in the town/city where the headquarters of the business are located) for a loan.

Tariq asks you to write a letter (which he will sign) to the bank manager. You decide to briefly outline Tariq's business proposition and ask for an appointment in the near future to discuss the matter.

Task 4
Before his appointment with the bank manager, Tariq asks you to help him prepare a statement of his financial position which will be helpful to the manager.

You are able to discover the following:
a) The current market value of the premises in ....(insert name of town/city where headquarters are located) is $62 000 (although Tariq only paid $40 000 several years ago).
b) The equipment and fixtures are in good condition and are valued at $11 000.
c) The current value of stock is $7400.
d) Creditors are owed $3800 and outstanding debts from customers amount to $4900.
e) The balance at bank amounts to $8100 and cash totals $630.
f) Tariq owns his own house (current market value is $71 000), but has an outstanding mortgage of $26 000.
g) Tariq has private investments amounting to $33 600.

Weighting
Task 1:   40%
Task 2:   10%
Task 3:   20%
Task 4:   30%

B Short assessments suitable for marking by students
Assessment 1
Suitable for use early in the course after introduction to Balance Sheets and double entry book-keeping

Time allowed: 20 minutes

1. L. Bashir had the following transactions. For each transaction indicate which account will be debited and which account will be credited.

	Transaction	Account to be debited	Account to be credited
a)	Bought goods on credit from M. Ali		
b)	M. Omar returned goods he had previously bought on credit		
c)	Paid surplus cash into the bank		
d)	L Bashir brought his own motor vehicle into the business		

(8)

2. a) Select the appropriate words and phrases from the following list and fill the spaces indicated by dotted lines in the Balance Sheet shown on page 76.

   for year ended   net profit   working capital
   as at   assets   liabilities
   long term   overdraft   drawings
   short term   creditors
   debtors   current

   b) Calculate the missing figures in the Balance Sheet, and insert in the spaces indicated by dotted lines.

Balance Sheet ....31 December 2003
$ $ $

Fixed ....
Premises   80 000
Fixtures   ....
                                                                      ....

.... Assets
Stock   5 800
....   3 600
Cash   ....
                                             9 000

Current ....
....   5 000
Bank...............   ....   7 600
                           ─────
....   1 400
                                                                      90 400

Capital
Opening balance   ....
Plus 23 400
                                                                      ....
Less 12 000
                                                                      83 400
........................Liabilities
Loan from ABC Finance   7 000
                                                                      90 400

(17)

3 A trader had the following transactions in January.
   a) Bought equipment on credit for $8000
   b) Received a cheque for $2000 from a debtor
   c) Paid wages in cash $1000
   d) Took $500 in cash for personal use
   e) Sold goods, $4000, on credit (the goods originally cost $3000)
   f) Half of the equipment bought for $8000 was unsuitable and was sold for $3000 cash

Complete the following table to show how each of the above transactions affect the assets, liabilities and capital of the trader. The first one has been completed as an example.

	Effect on assets	Effect on liabilities	Effect on capital
	Item + − $ $	Item + − $ $	+ − $ $
a)	Equipment 8000	Creditors 8000	No effect
b)			
c)			
d)			
e)			
f)			

(15)
(Total 40)

Assessment 2
Suitable for use after trial balances and books of original entry

Time allowed: 30 minutes

1 Insert the missing words in the following sentences.
  a) When a bank account is overdrawn it is shown as a .... in a Balance Sheet.
  b) Discounts received by a business from its suppliers appear as .... in a Profit and Loss Account.
  c) Carriage .... is always added to the purchases in a Trading Account.
  d) Amounts due for repayment after more than 12 months appear under the heading of .... in a Balance Sheet.
  e) A debit balance on a ledger account is either an .... or an ....

(6)

Appendix C: Examples of assessments 77

2. a) Give a definition of a trial balance
   ....
   ....

   b) What is the purpose of preparing a trial balance?
   ....
   ....

   c) Name three errors which would not be revealed by a trial balance and give an example of each.
      (i) Error ....
         Example ....
      (ii) Error ....
         Example ....
      (iii) Error ....
         Example ....
   (10)

3. Study the following account which appears in the ledger of Joe Blake and answer the following questions.

   Janet Jones account

2004		$	2004		$
Dec 1	Balance c/d	1000	Dec 6	Bank	950
17	Goods	3600	6	Discount	50
			21	Returns	80
			31	Balance c/d	3520
		4600			4600
2005					
Jan 1	Balance b/d	3520			

   a) On 1 December was Janet a debtor or a creditor of Joe?
   ....

   b) On 17 December did Janet purchase or sell goods?
   ....

   c) Who received the cheque on 6 December?
   ....

   d) What rate per cent of discount was allowed on 6 December?
   ....

   e) Was the discount on 6 December trade or cash discount?
   ....

   f) Will Janet regard the returns of 21 December as returns inwards or returns outwards?
   ....

g) In Joe's Balance Sheet on 31 December will the balance of $3520 appear as an asset or a liability?
   ....

h) If the debt owing on 1 January is paid by cheque on 7 January less a discount of $2\frac{1}{2}$%, what will be the amount of the cheque?
   ....

(8)

4 Martin is a trader, he keeps a full set of books of original entry. His transactions in February included the following.
   a) Paid window cleaner $10 out of petty cash
   b) Purchased goods for re-sale on credit from Alsorts $1620
   c) Sold goods for cash, $930 (the goods originally cost $810)
   d) Banked a cheque received from Sports & Co. for $1000
   e) Purchased a machine, $4600, on credit from Superquip

   (i) Complete the following table to show the book of original entry and the immediate or eventual ledger entries for the above transactions. The first one has been completed as an example.

Item	Book of original entry	Account to be debited	Account to be credited
a)	Petty cash book	Cleaning	Petty cash
b)			
c)			
d)			
e)			

(12)

(ii) Complete the following table to indicate how each of the above transactions will affect the working capital. The first has been completed as an example.

Item	Effect on Working Capital		
	Increase $	Decrease $	No effect
a)		10	
b)			
c)			
d)			
e)			

(4)
(Total 40)

C Longer assessments suitable for marking by the teacher
Assessment 1
Suitable for use after bank reconciliation and working capital

Time allowed: 20 minutes

a) On 1 January 2003 Mary, a trader, obtained a statement from her bank and compared it with the bank account in her cash book.
The bank balance shown in the cash book was an overdraft of $1780. This differed from the balance shown on the bank statement because:
  i) A cheque for $270 payable to David had not yet been presented for payment.
  ii) Cash paid into the bank amounting to $800 had not yet been credited to Mary's account.

Prepare a bank reconciliation statement to show the balance which appeared on the bank statement on 31 January 2003.

(4)

b) The following balances were extracted from the books of Mary at 31 January 2003:

	$
Machinery	26 000
Fixtures	8 500
Stock	6 600
Debtors	5 400
Creditors	4 620
Insurance prepaid	120
Rent received in advance	160
Bank overdraft	1 780
Cash	240
General expenses accrued	700
Long term loan	15 000
Capital	24 600

i) Select the relevant figures and calculate Mary's working capital on 31 January 2003.

(5)

ii) Calculate, correct to two decimal places, Mary's current ratio and quick ratio at 31 January 2003. Show your workings.

(4)

c) i) State and explain two disadvantages to a business of having insufficient working capital.

(4)

ii) State two ways in which a business could increase its working capital.

(4)

(IGCSE Paper 3 June 2003)

This assessment fulfils the following objectives on the IGCSE Accounting syllabus:

Core Syllabus	*Extended Syllabus*	*Skill A*	*Skill C*
13 marks	8 marks	9 marks	12 marks

Assessment 2
Suitable for use after journal entries and suspense accounts

Time allowed: 20 minutes

Maria Matsa's financial year ends on 30 September. The trial balance prepared on 30 September 2002 showed a shortage on the credit side of $788. Maria entered this in a suspense account and then prepared a draft Trading and Profit and Loss Account.

The following errors were later discovered:

1. $50 cash spent on stationery was entered in the cash book but not in the stationery account.
2. The sales journal was undercast by $1000.
3. $240 received from Abdul Ahmed, a customer, had been credited to the account of Adbulla Ahmed, another customer, in the sales ledger.
4. The total of the discount received column in the cash book of $14 had been debited to the discount allowed account in the general ledger.
5. $95 cash paid to Joe Jones, a trade creditor, had been credited to his account in the purchases ledger.

a) Prepare the entries in Maria Matsa's journal to correct the above errors. Narratives are not required. (11)

b) Prepare the suspense account in Maria Matsa's ledger to show the required amendments. Start with the balance arising from the difference on the trial balance. (6)

c) For each error 1–5 state how the draft net profit will be affected when the errors are corrected. If the error does not affect the draft net profit write 'no effect'.

The first one has been completed as an example.
Error 1   decrease by $50   (4)

(IGCSE Paper 3 November 2002)

This assessment fulfils the following objectives on the IGCSE Accounting syllabus:

Core Syllabus	Extended Syllabus	Skill B	Skill C
17 marks	4 marks	17 marks	4 marks

Appendix D: Key (command) words in Accounting examinations

advise Write down a suggested course of action in a given situation. Often linked with 'Suggest' – see below

calculate Work out. Often no format specified. Often accompanied by 'Show workings' or 'Show calculations'

comment Make relevant statements, usually on given figures or results of calculations

compare Write down the differences between two accounting statements or two businesses or two methods of recording something etc.

complete Fill in. Often used in relation to tables, sentences or 'boxes'.

define Write down an explanation of the meaning of an accounting term, e.g. 'Define depreciation' or 'Define current assets'

discuss Write down a reasoned explanation of the causes/effects of a course of action or the difference between two sets of figures or between two accounting statements etc. Often linked with 'Comment' – see above

draw up Present something in statement or account format etc. Sometimes used in place of 'Prepare'. Often used in relation to bank reconciliation or statement of corrected net profit etc

enter Record given information in specified accounts, books or ledgers. Sometimes used in place of 'Make entries'

explain Give a written account of what something means or why it is done or what the outcome is. Examples include 'Explain the entries in an account' or 'Explain why a trader …'

give Write down. Sometimes used in place of 'State'. Sometimes used as 'Give 2 examples …'

list Write down information in a number of points – usually no further explanation is necessary

make entries Record information in specified accounts etc. See 'Enter' above

name	Write down the name of ... Often used for short one-word answers, e.g. 'Name a fixed asset' or 'Name an example of ...'
outline	Give a brief written account of something, e.g. 'Outline the ways to reduce bad debts' or 'Outline the imprest system of petty cash'. Often linked to 'State' – see below
prepare	Present some accounting information in a suitable format, e.g. 'Prepare final accounts' or 'Prepare journal entries' or 'Prepare a bank reconciliation statement' – see 'Draw up' above
record	Make the necessary entries in a set of accounting records, e.g. 'Record a series of transactions in the cash book / ledger / books of prime entry'. Used in place of 'Enter' or 'Write up'
select	Choose relevant information from that given. Often linked to a further instruction, e.g. 'Select the relevant information and prepare a Manufacturing Account / Trial Balance'
show	Write down your workings/calculations or write down how an item will appear in an accounting statement. Often used when requiring preparation of Balance Sheet extracts or Profit and Loss Account extracts etc
state	Write down. Often used instead of 'Give' – see above. Used when requiring a written explanation of something, e.g. 'State 2 ways in which ...' or 'State how the trader can ...'
state and explain	Usually requires a little more detail than just 'State' and often an explanation of why/how
suggest	Offer an explanation of why something has occurred or how a situation can be improved or what methods are available to deal with a situation etc. Requires knowledge to be related to a given situation
using	Referring back to some previous information, e.g. 'Using your answer to Part (a), calculate / make suitable comments ...'
write up	Present accounting information in a suitable format. May be used in place of 'Prepare' – see above. Often used in connection with ledger accounts, cash books or books of prime entry

Appendix E: Answers to teacher activities

Teacher activity 2.7
- Knowledge with understanding
- Analysis
- Knowledge with understanding
- Evaluation
- Analysis
- Evaluation

Teacher activity 2.8
a) Skill B
b) Skill A
c) Skill C
d) Skill C

Teacher activity 5.4
- Correct figure (or correct figure only)
- Own figure
- Own figure provided that the accounting statement does not contain items which should not be included
- Duplicated item, e.g. where an entry appears on both sides of a ledger account
- Repetition, e.g. where two statements say the same thing using different words

Teacher activity 5.5
a) Prudence or Matching (Accruals) [1]
b) Bad debts – amounts owing to a business which it considers will never be paid (1)
Provision for doubtful debts – an estimate by a business of the likely amount of debtors who will not be able to pay their accounts (1)
[2]

c) 1 Look at each debtor's account and estimate which will not be paid
2 Estimate, on the basis of past experience, what percentage of debtors will prove to be bad debts
3 Make use of an ageing schedule
Any two points (1) each [2]

d) (i)

Bad debts account

2004		$	2004		$
Mar 31	Debtors written off	800 **(1)**	Mar 31	Profit & Loss	800 **(1)**
		800			800

Provision for doubtful debts account

2004		$	2003		$
Mar 31	Balance c/d	1150 **(1)**	Apr 1	Balance	1000 **(2)**
			2004		
			Mar 31	Profit & Loss	150 **(1)O/F**
		1150			1150
			2004		
			Apr 1	Balance b/d	1150 **(1)O/F**

Plus (1) for dates (both accounts)

[8]

See end of answer for alternative presentation of (d)(i)

(ii)

Mary Maranga
Extract from Balance Sheet as at 31 March 2004

	$	$
Current Assets **(1)**		
Debtors	46 000 **(1)**	
Less: Provision for doubtful debts	1 150 **(1)O/F**	44 850 **(1)O/F** [4]

e)
1. Obtain credit references for new credit customers
2. Set a credit limit for each debtor
3. Issue invoices and statements promptly
4. Follow up over-due accounts promptly
5. Supply goods on a cash-only basis (or reduce credit sales)
6. Refuse further supplies until outstanding debts are paid

Or other suitable points

Any 3 points (1) each [3]

[Total 20]

d) (i) Alternative presentation

Bad debts account

2004		Debit $	Credit $	Balance $
Mar 31	Debtors written off	800 **(1)**		800
	Profit & Loss		800 **(1)**	

Provision for doubtful debts account

		Debit $	Credit $	Balance $
2003				
April 1	Balance		1000 **(2)**	1000
2004				
Mar 31	Profit & Loss		150 **(1) O/F**	1150 **(1) O/F** **(2) C/F**

Plus **(1)** for dates (both accounts)

[8]

Teacher activity 5.6
- Stem – the question
- Options – the four answers from which students have to select the correct one
- Key – the option which is correct
- Distractors – the options which are incorrect

Teacher activity 5.7
1 The key could be either B or D depending on whether a business lists them in increasing or decreasing order of liquidity.
2 The options are not listed alphabetically, but, more importantly, distractors B and C are basically the same thing.
3 This would be regarded as too long and complex for inclusion. Additionally, it is a negative question which should preferably be avoided. Also, one option is much shorter than the other three.

Index

accounting statements,
    interpretation of 44–6
advertisements 8
assessing skills 51–60
assessing your own performance
    11–12
assessment aims 13
assessment objectives 14–16
assessments
    'cross-subject' 29, 73–4
    examples of 73–82
    formative 51–4
    suitable for marking by students
        75–80
    suitable for marking by the
        teacher 80–2
    summative 54–8

bank reconciliation statements
    (lesson plan) 32–4
business work experience 9–10

calculators, use of 23
class, how to keep working at
    same pace 48–9
classroom facilities 3
colleagues, observing lessons of 9
command words 61, 83–4
creditors' payment period 27–8
'cross-subject' assessments 29,
    73–4

debtors' collection period 27–8
depreciation of fixed assets
    (lesson plan) 36–7
display boards 3, 7
double entry book-keeping
    1, 18, 48
    assignment example 40–1

errors
    not revealed by a trial balance
        42–3
    using as teaching points 44
external examination papers
    marking 55–6
    setting 54–5
external examinations
    examiners' reports 10, 62–3
    hints for students 64–5
    preparing students for 61–7
    topics students have problems
        with 38
    ways marks can be lost 22, 66–7

feedback, from assessments 53
films 8–9
final accounts, interpretation of
    44–6
fixed assets, depreciation of
    (lesson plan) 36–7
formative assessments 51–4
    feedback from 53

formative assessments (*cont.*)
   marking 52
   planning 51
   setting 53–4

guest speakers 9

handouts 7

integrating skills 28–30
internal examination papers
   marking 56–8
   setting 55
interpretation of accounting statements 44–6

journal entries 38

key words 61, 83–4

language skills 24–5
learning activities 46–8
learning by rote 25, 42
learning environment 3
learning skills 25–6
ledger accounts, closing of 38, 39
lesson plans 32–7
   bank reconciliation statements 32–4
   depreciation of fixed assets 36–7
   partnerships 34–5
lesson record sheets 11–12
lessons
   basic elements 31
   keeping students working at similar pace 48–9
   preparation of adequate amount of material 48–50
   preparation of 5–6
   varying activities of 5, 46
   varying format of 32–7

mark schemes 10, 22, 56, 57

marking
   external examination papers 55–6
   formative assessments 52
   internal examination papers 56–8
mixed-ability teaching 48
mnemonics 25–6
multiple-choice questions 58–60

newspapers 8
numerical skills 23

online resources 10–11
outside visits 30
overhead projectors 7

Pacioli, Luca 1
partnerships (lesson plan) 34–5
periodicals 8
performance, assessing your own 11
petty cash book, posting of analysis columns to ledger accounts 38
posters 7–8
PowerPoint presentations 7
practical skills 21–2
presentation errors 22
professional development 9
professional publications 11

reasoning skills 27–8
resources 4
   for students 6–9
   for teachers 9–11
revision strategies 63–4

scheme of work 31
   converting syllabus into 16–19
   example of 17
   planning 5
   preparation of detailed 19

skills
- assessing 51–60
- integrating 28–30
- language 24–5
- learning 25–6
- methods of teaching accounting 31–50
- numerical 23
- practical 21–2
- reasoning 27–8

Standards Booklet 62
stationery, accounting 4
students
- answering their questions 49
- device to keep working at same pace 48–9
- talking to individual 6

summative assessment 54–8
syllabus 5
- aims and objectives 13
- converting into scheme of work 16–19
- interpreting the 13–16

syllabus support materials 61–2

technical words or phrases 24

textbooks 4, 6–7, 10, 69–70
topics
- interrelationship of 37–41
- teaching order 16–18
- trial balance, errors not revealed by 42–3

understanding vs. learning by rote 42

videos 8–9

wall charts 7–8
websites 10–11, 71–2
working capital cycle 28

Other titles in the Professional Development for Teachers series

Teaching and Assessing Skills in Computer Studies	0 521 75360 0
Teaching and Assessing Skills in First Language English	0 521 75355 4
Teaching and Assessing Skills in Mathematics	0 521 75361 9
Teaching and Assessing Skills in Geography	0 521 75357 0
Teaching and Assessing Practical Skills in Science	0 521 75359 7
Teaching and Assessing Skills in English as Second Language	0 521 75356 2
Teaching and Assessing Skills in History	0 521 75358 9
Teaching and Assessing Skills in Foreign Languages	0 521 60103 7
Teaching and Assessing Skills in Economics	0 521 54825 X
Teaching and Assessing Skills in Business Studies	0 521 54366 5